Essential
Windows 10
April 2018 Edition

Kevin Wilson

Elluminet Press

www.elluminetpress.com

Essential Windows 10: April 2018 Edition

Publisher: Elluminet Press
Director: Kevin Wilson
Lead Editor: Steven Ashmore
Technical Reviewer: Mike Taylor, Robert Ashcroft
Copy Editors: Joanne Taylor, James Marsh
Proof Reader: Mike Taylor
Indexer: James Marsh
Cover Designer: Kevin Wilson

eBook versions and licenses are also available for most titles. Any source code or other supplementary materials referenced by the author in this text is available to readers at

`www.elluminetpress.com/resources`

For detailed information about how to locate your book's source code, go to

`www.elluminetpress.com/resources`

Table of Contents

About the Author

Kevin Wilson has made a career out of technology and showing others how to use it. After earning a master's degree in computer science, software engineering, and multimedia systems, Kevin worked as a tutor and college instructor, helping students master such subjects as multimedia, computer literacy and information technology. He currently serves as Elluminet Press Publishing's senior writer and director, he periodically teaches computing at college in South Africa and serves as an IT trainer in England.

Kevin's motto is clear: "If you can't explain something simply, you haven't understood it well enough." To that end, he has created the Computer Essentials series, in which he breaks down complex technological subjects into smaller, easy-to-follow steps that students and ordinary computer users can put into practice.

Have fun.

Acknowledgements

Thanks to all the staff at Luminescent Media & Elluminet Press for their passion, dedication and hard work in the preparation and production of this book.

To all my friends and family for their continued support and encouragement in all my writing projects.

To all my colleagues, students and testers who took the time to test procedures and offer feedback on the book

Finally thanks to you the reader for choosing this book. I hope it helps you to use your computer with greater understanding.

Windows 10

Windows 10 is known as an Operating System. An Operating System is a computer program that manages the computer's hardware resources such as memory, processor and disk drives. The Operating System also provides a platform for you to run applications such as word processors, web browsers, games and so on.

These days, computing falls into two categories: creators and consumers.

Creators usually use desktop PCs to write books, papers, edit videos, create graphics, edit photos, websites or blogs. They use a keyboard and mouse on a point and click desktop environment, however more recently, this has begun to include touch screen devices using pens with graphic tablets and so on.

Consumers usually use laptops, tablets or smart phones to read or type emails, post on social media, browse the web, stream movies or tv, look at photographs, listen to music, play a few games, maybe even type a document or spreadsheet. They tend to use a touch screen environment, especially on tablets and smart phones, or a combination of both touch screen and mouse on laptops.

To address this user divide, Microsoft designed Windows 10 to run on and adapt to these different devices.

Windows Editions

There are two editions of Windows 10 available to consumers: Home and Pro.

Windows 10 Home is designed for use on PCs, laptops and tablets. This edition is intended for the every day home user.

Windows 10 Pro is the same as the home edition, except it has additional features that are oriented towards business environments and power users.

Microsoft subsequently released other editions of Windows 10 aimed at different markets.

Windows 10 Enterprise is aimed at medium to large scale organisations that have hundreds or even thousands of computers in their offices and networks. This edition is very similar to Windows 10 Pro except it has a couple of extra features.

Windows 10 Education is very much like Windows 10 Pro and Windows 10 Enterprise but is distributed to educational establishments such as schools, colleges, and universities.

Windows 10 S is a feature-limited edition of Windows 10 designed primarily for low-end devices and the education market. Windows 10 S only allows the installation of software from the Windows Store. You can only use Microsoft Edge as the web browser and Bing as the search engine.

Windows 10 Pro for Workstations is designed for high-end hardware for intensive computing tasks and supports Intel Xeon or AMD Opteron processors, up to 4 CPUs, 6TB RAM, the ReFS file system.

The April 2018 Update

Windows 10 April 2018 Update, also known as Redstone 4, is the latest update to Windows 10 after the Fall Creator's Update released at the end of 2017. Microsoft releases major updates to Windows 10 twice a year, one in April and one in October.

Microsoft originally released the Creator's Update series at content creators, with the introduction of Paint 3D that includes new tools to create 3D models and 3D scenes. Windows 10 is not just for creators and still comes with a wealth of features for home and business users.

The April 2018 Update introduces some new features while continually improving others. Lets take a look at some of the newest features.

The task view button has been replaced with Timeline, allowing you to view your activity history

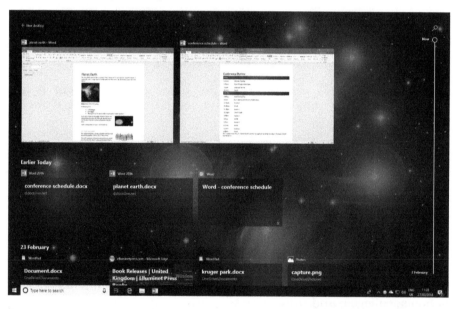

Cloud Clipboard allows you to copy and paste information across all your devices, eg copy a phone number or message from your phone and paste it into a document on your laptop

Near Share allows you to share files and images with devices in the save vicinity using bluetooth.

Story Remix 3D has been added to the Photos App and now includes various kinds of 3D effects that can be added to your movies.

The Settings App has had a few visual improvements with some more options added. You can now manage your system fonts as well as download new ones from the Windows Store.

Sound and display settings are now available in the Settings App giving you greater control over system sounds, monitors, graphics card and screen resolutions. Game-specific graphics options are now in the Settings App.

A new privacy section has been added allowing you to control what personal information Windows 10 saves.

There is a new section in the Settings App that allows you to block startup apps from running when you power up your PC.

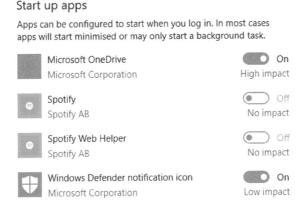

The new Game Bar has a clock and buttons for taking screenshots, recording video clips and turning Game Mode on and off.

If you ever forget your password, you can now reset it from the lock screen.

The Action Center, Start Menu, calendar and settings areas use Microsoft's latest fluent design.

Chapter 2

Setting up Windows 10

Most new devices and computers will come with Windows 10 already installed. If you are running and older system such as Windows 7 or Windows 8 you should upgrade your system to Windows 10.

Microsoft's free upgrade may be over, but since they want as many people on Windows 10 as possible, those with activated versions of Windows 7 and Windows 8 can still upgrade for free. If you are running either of those two operating systems, you should upgrade as soon as possible.

In this chapter we'll take a look at how to upgrade - you can do this using the media creation tool, available from Microsoft's website.

We'll also take a look at running Windows 10 for the first time as well as setting it up, installing printers, connecting to WiFi and Windows 10's many other features.

Upgrading to Windows 10

If you have a fully licensed version of Windows 7 or 8 installed on your machine, you can still upgrade for free using the Media Creation Tool - see section on upgrading from Windows 7 & 8.

If you're upgrading, make sure your PC meets the following specification. A computer with the minimum spec recommended by Microsoft will run painfully slow, so I've included a recommended minimum spec in brackets that I've had Windows 10 running smoothly.

- 1GHz or faster CPU (2GHz min recommended)
- At least 2GB of RAM (4GB min recommended)
- At least 20GB Hard Disk Space (500GB min recommended)
- 800x600 screen resolution (1152x864 min recommended)
- Graphics card with WDDM support and DirectX 9 or above.

If you Already have Windows 10

If you are already running Windows 10 and simply want to get the Spring Creator's Update, then you should automatically receive a notification on Windows Update.

Go to Start -> Settings App, Update & Security -> Windows Update. Click 'check for updates'.

Windows 10 will check and download any available updates. The spring creator's update is version 1803. The update will download and install automatically.

To complete the update, you'll need to restart your machine when it's finished. Go to Start > Power > 'Update & Restart'. If you only see 'restart' on the menu, then the update hasn't finished downloading yet.

Buying Windows 10

If you can't upgrade free for whatever reason, you can buy Windows 10 from any computer store or online retailer. The installation media for Windows 10 will either come as a download, a DVD disk or a flash/usb drive.

The best place is to buy a copy from Microsoft's Online Store, using your Microsoft Account. Head over to the following website.

        www.microsoftstore.com/windows

Scroll down and click 'Windows 10 Home', or 'Windows 10 Pro', for most users the home edition is fine.

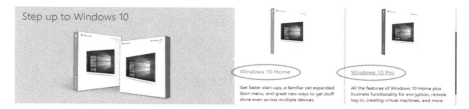

Select 'how do you want to get Windows 10'. You can select either Download disk image or a USB stick. Having Windows 10 installer on a USB stick is useful for installing and is easier to use than a disk image.

Windows 10 Home

Windows 10 is your partner in making things happen. Get fast start-ups, a familiar yet expanded Start menu, and great new ways to get stuff done even across multiple devices. You'll also love the innovative features like an all-new browser built for online action, plus Cortana, the personal digital assistant who helps you across your day. Windows 10 is not compatible with Windows Vista.

How do you want to get Windows 10? **USB Flash Drive**

Download	USB Flash Drive

Quantity: | 1 ▾ |

Buy Windows 10 (USB Flash Drive)

Click 'buy and download'.

You'll see a summary of your order and how much it is going to cost. Click 'checkout', when you're happy.

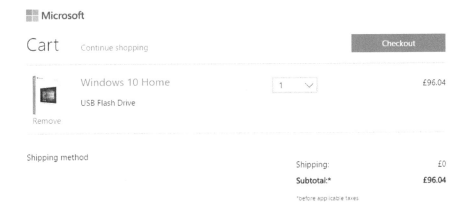

Click 'sign in and checkout'. Sign in with your Microsoft Account email address and password.

Run through the steps to enter payment details and confirm order. You'll be able to download Windows 10 and Microsoft will send you a copy on a USB stick.

This will associate your Windows 10 license with your Microsoft Account and the device you're installing it on. This means that when you log into Windows 10 with your Microsoft Account email address and password, Windows will automatically activate on your device, even if you have to re-install Windows.

To install Windows 10, insert the USB stick, open up your file explorer, navigate to the USB stick and run the 'setup.exe' file; see next section. You can also upgrade using the Media Creation Tool; see page 32.

If your device, laptop or PC came with Windows 10, you don't need to buy a copy, unless for example, you have Windows 10 Home and want to upgrade to Windows 10 Pro.

Upgrading from Windows 7 & 8

At the time of writing, if you have an activated version of Windows 7 or Windows 8, you can still upgrade to Windows 10 for free. To do this, go to the following website and download the media creation tool.

`www.microsoft.com/software-download/windows10`

Double click on mediacreationtool.exe, or click 'run' when prompted by your browser. If you don't see it, the file will be in your downloads folder on your file explorer.

On the opening blue screen, make sure 'upgrade this PC now' is selected and click 'next'.

Follow the instructions on screen. Leave the setting selected; 'download and install updates'. This will insure you get the latest release of Windows 10. Click 'next'.

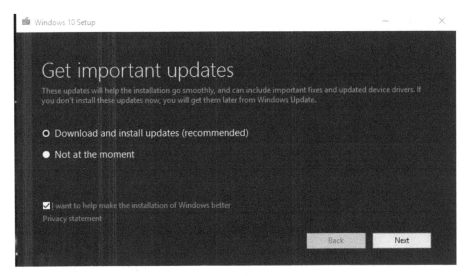

Click 'Accept' to accept the licence terms.

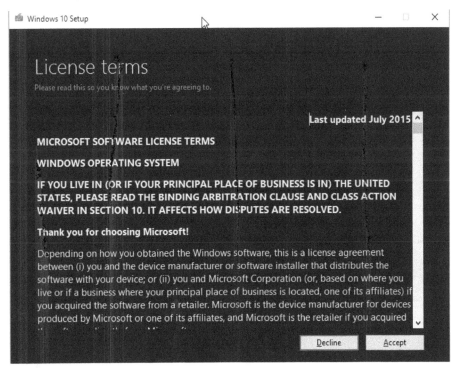

Chapter 2: Setting up Windows 10

On the next screen, choose what data you want to keep. You have three options.

Keep personal files, apps and Windows settings

This upgrades everything to Windows 10 and transfers all your installed apps, settings and personal files.

Keep personal files only

Use this option if you want to remove installed apps, old windows settings and applications but keep all your personal files. If you choose this option you will need to re-install your applications.

Keep Nothing

This will wipe all your files, applications and settings. Only do this if you have backed up all your personal files. Useful if you want a fresh install of Windows 10.

If in doubt click 'keep personal files, apps and windows settings' to keep everything. This will keep all your files, any compatible applications and windows settings such as Edge/Explorer browser histories, contacts, desktop themes/backgrounds and so on.

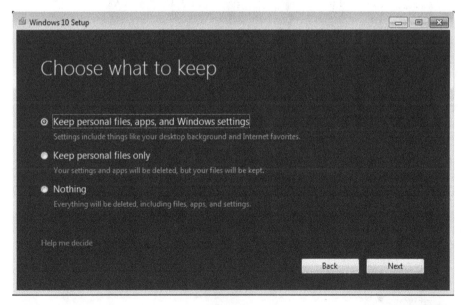

Click Next.

Windows will shut down and restart. Once restarted windows update will kick in and configure the updates. This will take a while.

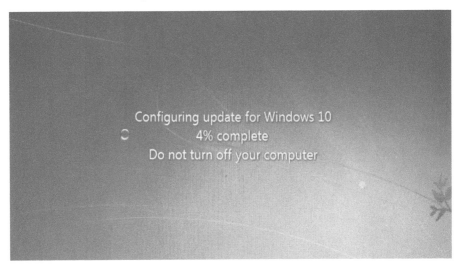

Setup will restart and Windows will proceed with the install. This will also take a while.

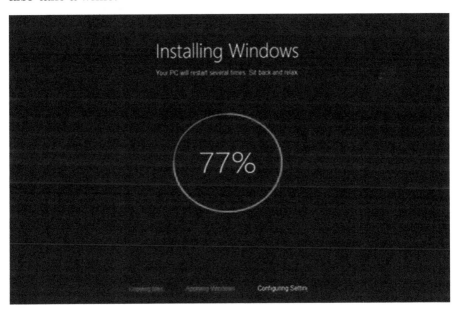

Once Windows 10 is installed, you'll see the 'welcome to windows 10' screen.

Chapter 2: Setting up Windows 10

Welcome to Windows 10. You will notice Windows 10 has imported your username from Windows 7/8. Click next.

Select 'use express settings' to let Windows 10 use the default settings.

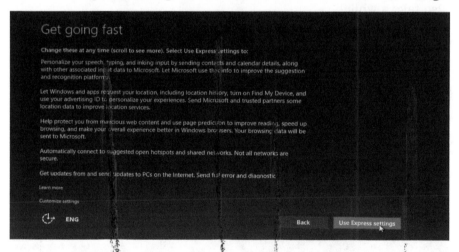

Click next on the following screen. Windows will start to configure itself and restart. Once it restarts you will land on the new Windows 10 desktop. You may need to go through 'running windows the first time' section, if you selected 'keep nothing' and decided to do a fresh install.

Upgrading from Windows 8 the same procedure.

Once you see the desktop you should switch to your Microsoft Account if Windows doesn't do it for you.

To check, go to the start menu and select settings on the bottom left.

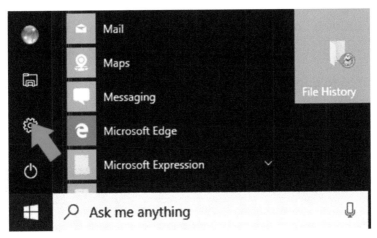

From the settings dialog box that appears, select accounts. If you see 'Local Account' then click 'Sign in with a Microsoft Account'.

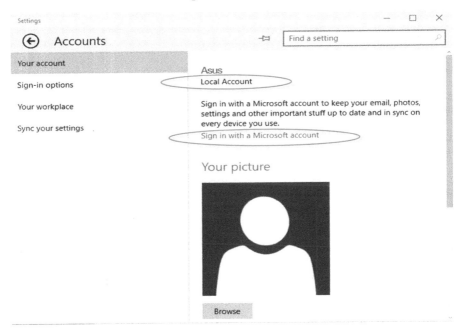

If you see 'Microsoft Account', you don't need to do anything here and can skip this step.

Update Assistant

The Update Assistant downloads and installs the latest version of Windows 10.

Open your web browser and navigate to the following website.

`www.microsoft.com/software-download/windows10`

You'll need to purchase a license from the Microsoft Store, if you don't already have one. On the webpage click 'update now'.

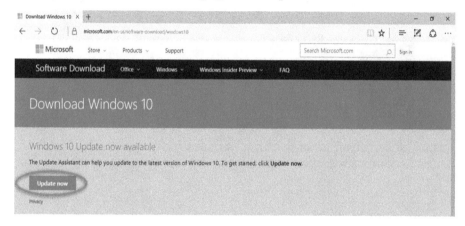

Click 'run' when prompted by your browser

Once the update assistant starts, click 'update now'.

Update Assistant will do a check on your device to make sure it is able to run the update. Click 'next' when the check is complete.

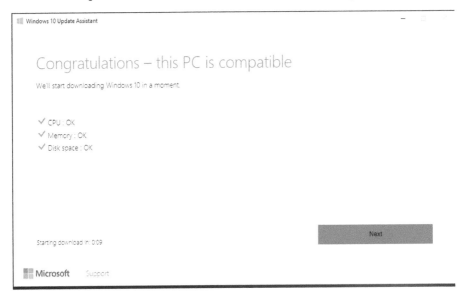

The Update Assistant will now download and install the update. You can leave the Update Assistant open or you can minimise it and carry on working. To minimise the assistant and run it in the background, click 'minimise'.

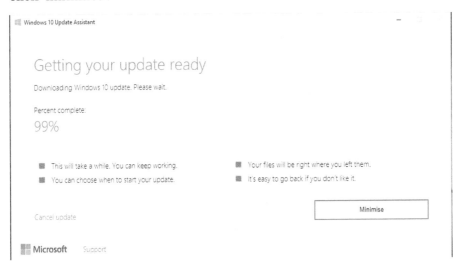

Once the update has been configured, click 'restart now'. You'll also notice a countdown on the left hand side of the screen. This means your device will restart automatically when the countdown hits zero.

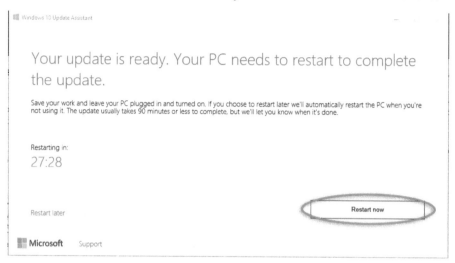

Your device will restart and installation will begin. This can take a while to complete.

Once the installation is complete, you'll need to run through some settings.

You can turn them all on, but keep diagnostic information to 'basic', then click 'accept'. Select your username, if there is more than one, then click 'next'.

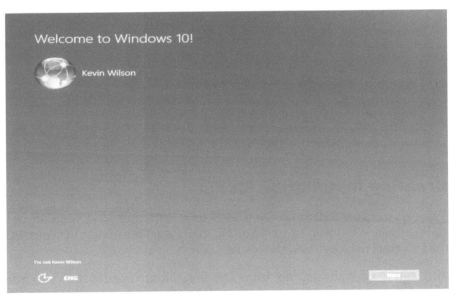

Click 'next' on the following screen. You can then log in when prompted.

Media Creation Tool

Microsoft has released a tool that you can download and run on your computer. This will allow you to create an install DVD or USB stick. These can be useful if your machine fails or has problems and will allow you to reinstall Windows 10 on your PC.

Open your web browser and navigate to the following website. You'll need to purchase a license from the Microsoft Store, if you don't already have one.

www.microsoft.com/software-download/windows10

Scroll down the page and at the bottom click 'download tool now'.

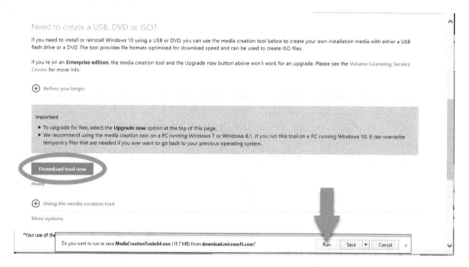

Click 'run' when prompted by your browser. Once the tool has download, it will run.

Creating Installation Media

You can use this tool to create a DVD or a USB stick that you can use to re-install Windows 10 on your PC. This media is useful if your PC fails to start or your hard disk fails.

You can start your PC up from the installation media and run the installation process again to restore your computer.

To create the installation media, we are going to use a USB stick. Make sure your USB stick is at least 8GB.

First, plug your USB stick into your PC.

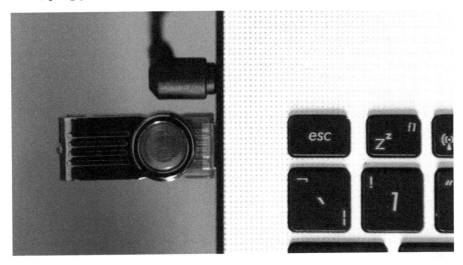

From the media creation tool, select 'create installation media for another PC'

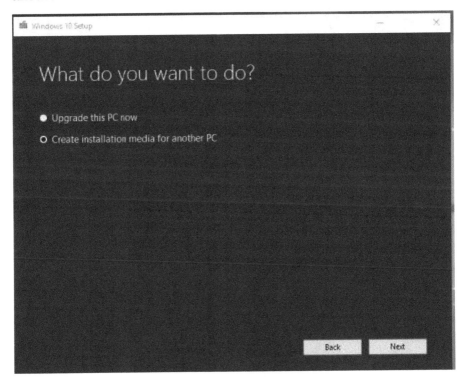

Click Next.

Chapter 2: Setting up Windows 10

Select your language, edition of Windows 10 (home or pro) and your computer's architecture (either 32bit for older machines and 64bit for machines purchased in the last 5-10 years).

Most of the time, the media creation tool will automatically select these settings based on your current version of windows and hardware.

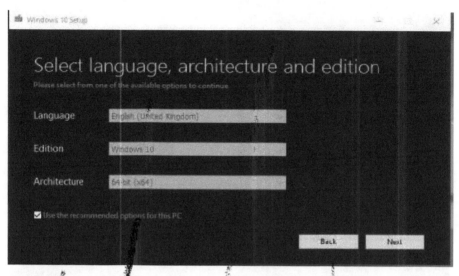

Click next.

Select your installation media. In this case, we are using a USB stick, so select 'USB flash drive'.

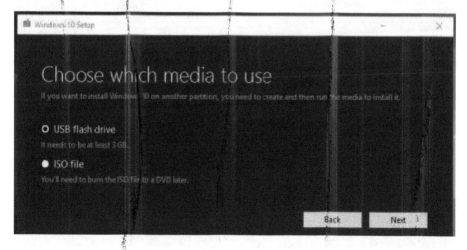

Click next.

34

The media creation tool will scan for your USB stick and will display what it finds in the next window.

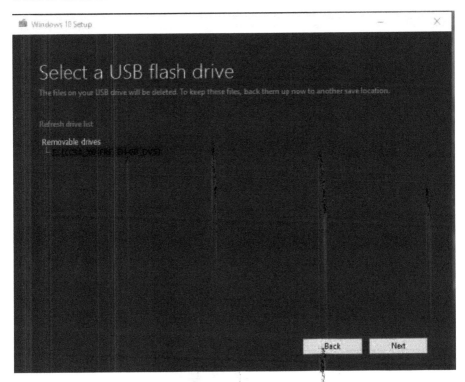

Click next to start the process.

This process can take a while depending on the speed of your PC. Once it has finished, store your USB stick in a safe place, as you probably won't need it unless you have problems or want to install a fresh copy of Windows 10.

If you run into problems with your PC, you can always start it up using the USB stick you just created.

Media Creation Tool to Upgrade your PC

Download and run the Media Creation tool from the following website. You'll need to purchase a license from the Microsoft Store, if you don't already have one.

```
www.microsoft.com/software-download/windows10
```

From the main screen click 'upgrade this PC now'.

Click Next

Windows 10 installation files will be downloaded. This may take a while depending on your internet connection speed.

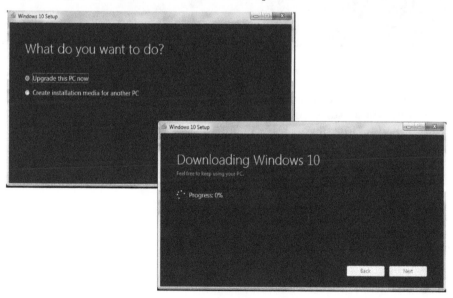

Once downloaded, the creation tool will verify the download for errors, create the installer and check for updates. Click next. Again, this can take a while...

Accept the license terms. Windows creation tool will now download any updates it needs to install.

Click 'change what to keep'. Click 'keep personal files only' if you want to remove installed apps but keep all your personal files, removing all old windows settings and applications. If you choose this option you will need to re-install your applications.

Selecting 'keep nothing' will wipe all your files, applications and settings. Only do this if you have backed up all your personal files.

If in doubt click 'keep personal files, apps and windows settings' to keep everything.

Click Next.

Once Windows is ready, click install. Windows will start the install. Your machine will restart a few times before it sorts itself out.

Windows will run you through the initial setup; running windows the first time.

Running Windows the First Time

If you've just bought a new computer with Windows 10, or just installed a fresh copy, you'll need to run through the initial set up procedure.

Regional Settings

Select your country or region from the list and click 'yes'.

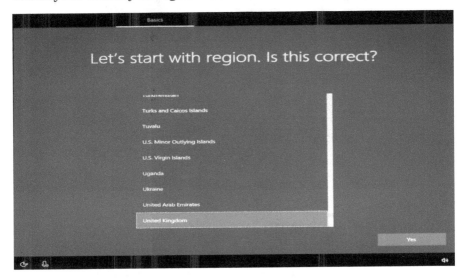

Select keyboard layout for your country, then click 'yes'. Skip secondary keyboard if you don't have one.

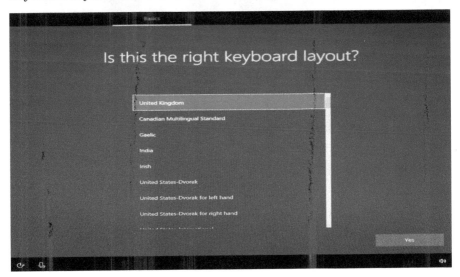

Terms Of Use

On the terms and agreements page click on 'Accept'.

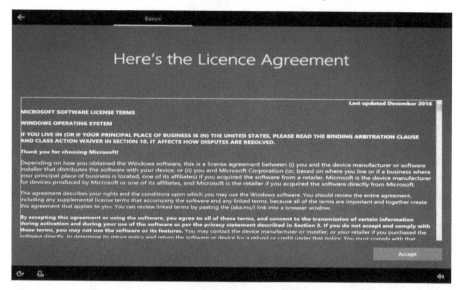

Connect to your WiFi

Select your WiFi network from the list of detected networks. This is usually printed on your router/modem or you can find out from your service provider. Click 'connect' from the box that appears.

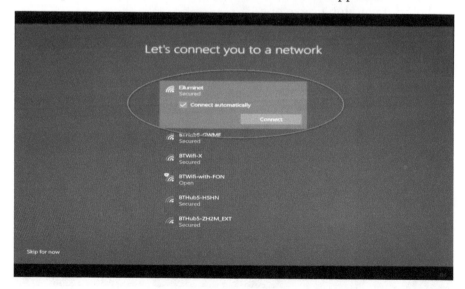

Enter WiFi Password

Enter the password for your WiFi network. This will be printed on the back of your router/modem, or you can find out from your service provider.

Click 'yes' to the prompt if you are on your home WiFi network. Click 'no' if you're using a public wifi hotspot such as a library, coffee shop or airport - you don't want other people to see you on a public network.

Sign in for the First Time

Sign in with your Microsoft Account email address and password, then click 'next'. This allows you to make use of OneDrive, email, purchase apps from the App Store, buy music and films.

If you don't have one, click 'create one', and fill in the form.

Set a PIN Code

Click 'Set a PIN code', then tap in your code, if you want the extra security. This means you can enter a 4 digit pin code instead of a password. If you prefer typing a password click 'do this later'.

Set up OneDrive

OneDrive is your online storage where you can store your files and access them from any of your devices. Click 'yes' to enable OneDrive.

Meet Cortana

Here you can enable your digital assistant and use voice commands.

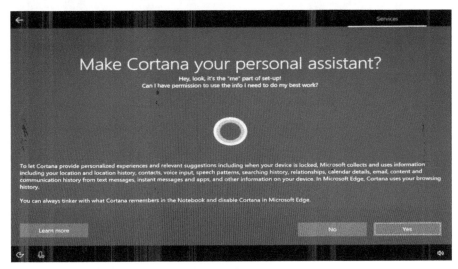

Click 'yes' to enable Cortana, or click 'no' if you can't be bothered talking to your computer.

Privacy Settings

I find it useful to turn the diagnostics to 'basic', turn off 'tailored experiences with diagnostic data' and turn off 'relevant ads'. This helps maximise your privacy and limits data sent to Microsoft.

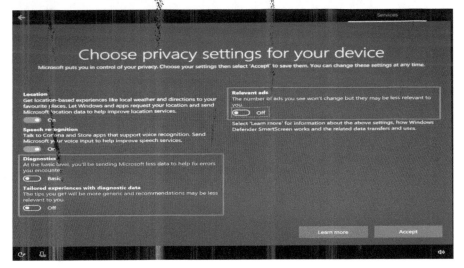

Chapter 2: Setting up Windows 10

Once Windows has all your preferences and details, it will configure your computer. Time for a coffee... this will take a while.

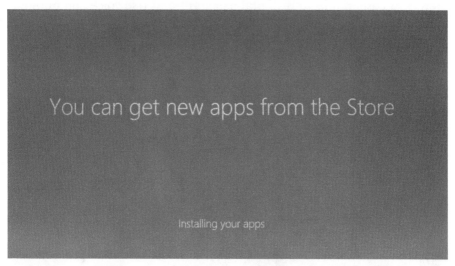

Once the configuration is complete, you'll land on the Windows 10 desktop.

We'll take a look at this in Chapter 3.

Verifying Accounts

If you have signed into a new computer with your Microsoft Account, you'll need to verify your identity on that new computer. This is done as a security procedure.

To do this, go to the Settings App and click 'accounts'.

If you see 'you need to verify your identity on this PC', then you need to run through the verification process. Click 'verify'.

Enter the recovery email address you added when you signed up for your Microsoft Account. Click 'next'.

Check the recovery email account and enter the code from the 'Microsoft Account Team' email message. Click 'Next' to finish.

Settings App

User settings can be found by clicking 'settings' on the bottom left of the start menu.

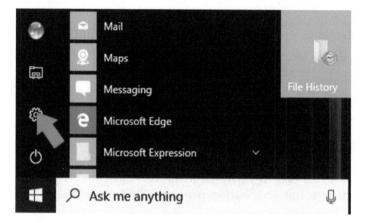

Here you'll see a window with different categories. Settings for different features and options are grouped into these categories.

For example, all settings to do with devices such as printers, mice and keyboards can be found in the devices category. All system settings are found in the system category. Windows updates, backup and security settings are found in the update & security category.

Here's a summary of the different options you have.

System
Display, notifications & actions, power & sleep, battery, storage, tablet mode, multitasking, projecting to this PC, shared experiences and about this computer.

Devices
Bluetooth & devices, printers & scanners, mouse, typing, pen & ink, autoplay, USB.

Phone
Link your iPhone or Android phone here.

Network & Internet
Network status, WiFi, dialup, VPN, flight mode, mobile hotspot, data usage and proxy servers.

Personalisation
Desktop background, colour schemes, lock screen, themes, start menu, taskbar.

Apps
Apps & features, default apps, offline maps, apps for websites, block start up apps.

Accounts
Your account settings, email & accounts, sign in options, connect to work or school network, family & other people, sync settings across devices.

Time & Language
Set date and time, region & language, text to speech settings.

Gaming
Game bar, game DVR, broadcasting, game mode settings.

Ease of Access
On-screen narrator, magnifier, high contrast, closed captions, keyboard accessibility, mouse pointers and other visual & audio options.

Cortana
Customise Cortana, change her language, preferences and settings.

Privacy
General privacy, location, camera, microphone, notifications, speech & inking, account info, contacts, calendar, call history, email, tasks, messaging, radios, feedback, background apps, app diagnostics.

Update & Security
Windows update, windows defender, backup, troubleshooting, Windows recovery, activation, find my device, developer settings.

Chapter 2: Setting up Windows 10

The quickest way to change a setting is to search for it using the search field on the settings app.

For example, if I wanted to change the printer settings, I could just type 'printer' into the search field where it says 'find a setting'.

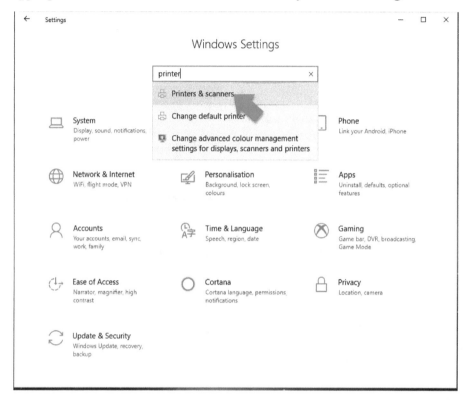

Double click on 'Printers & Scanners'.

You can do this for any setting you need to change.

Connecting to WiFi Networks

To locate nearby WiFi networks, tap the WiFi icon on the bottom right of the screen or open the action centre and tap 'network'.

   or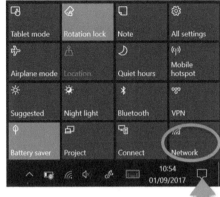

Tap the name of the network you want to join, then tap 'connect'

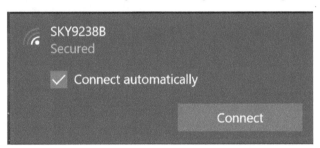

Enter the WiFi password or network key.

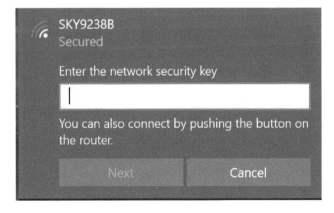

Once you have done that tap 'next' or 'ok'.

For your home WiFi, the network key or password is usually printed on the back of your router.

Sometimes the network name is called an SSID.

Use the same procedure if you are on a public hotspot such as in a cafe, library, hotel, airport and so on. You'll need to find the network key if they have one. Some are open networks and you can just connect.

When using public hotspots, keep in mind that most of them don't encrypt the data you send over the internet and aren't secure. So don't start checking your online banking account or shop online while using an unsecured connection, as anyone who is on the public wifi hotspot potentially can gain access to anything you do

If you're really concerned about security or use your devices on public hotspots for work, then you should consider a VPN or Virtual Private Network. A VPN essentially encrypts all the data you send and receive over a network. There are a few good ones to choose from, some have a free option with a limited amount of data and others you pay a subscription.

Take a look at www.tunnelbear.com, windscribe.com & speedify.com

To set up a VPN, open Action Centre > VPN > Add VPN Connection

Enter the connection details from one of the VPN providers above.

Setting up Additional Users

You can set up multiple users for different people on your computer. This will allow them to use their own personal account and have access to their own OneDrive, calendar or email.

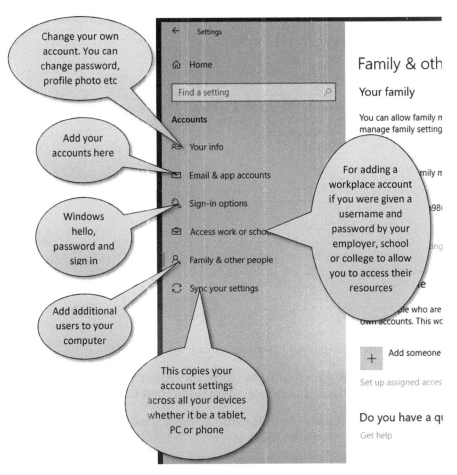

Users can have different privileges: Administrator and Standard

Administrators have complete access to your computer and can install software and change settings. Administrator accounts should only be used to change settings and install software, not for everyday computing.

Standard users can use apps and make limited changes to the system settings and are best for everyday computing needs.

Child users are monitored and reported to an 'adult' user.

Adding a New User

To add a new user, from the start menu, select Settings App.

From the Settings App select 'accounts'.

Select 'Family & other people'.

Click 'Add someone else to this PC'.

Enter the user's Microsoft account email address.

If they don't have one, click 'I don't have the person's sign-in information' and enter their details to create them a Microsoft Account.

The new user will be able to log into Windows with their own account and can select it from the login screen.

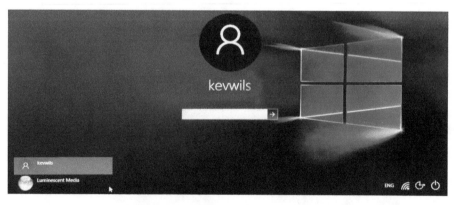

Family Safety

You can create child accounts for your children either on your devices or their own devices. These are special, restricted accounts you can monitor and tailor to your child. It is not a good idea to allow a young child to use your account.

Child Accounts

On your child's computer or tablet, sign in as an administrator (your own account). Open the Settings App and click 'accounts'. Select 'family & other people' on the left hand side, click 'add a family member'.

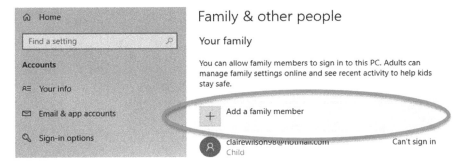

Select 'add a child' and enter their email address.

Click 'next', then 'confirm'. This will send an invitation to join to the child's email address.

If they don't have an email address, click 'the person who I want to add doesn't have an email address' and create them a Microsoft Account email address and password.

Chapter 2: Setting up Windows 10

Children's accounts give parents the ability to block certain services or monitor their child's online activity.

Sign out of your account, then sign in with the Microsoft Account username and password you just added/created for your child.

A confirmation email will be sent the child's email address inviting them to sign in.

Open the email app. You'll see an email from 'Microsoft Family'. Open the email and click 'accept invitation'.

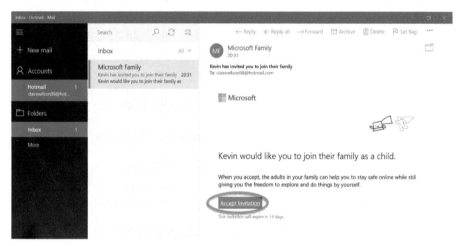

On the page that appears, click 'sign in and join'.

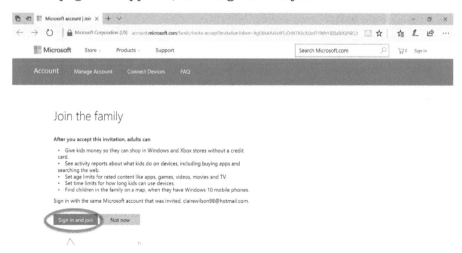

The child account will now be in the family settings on your own account.

Monitoring Family Activity

You can log on to your family safety website by opening your web browser and navigating to the following address. Click 'sign in' and enter your Microsoft Account email address and password.

```
account.microsoft.com/family
```

On the main family screen you'll see a list of child accounts.

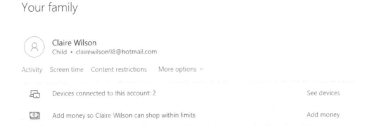

Under their name you'll see 'activity'. This shows web activity and apps used. Screen Time, allows you to set limits and curfews to control how long your child uses the computer and times they are allowed access. Content restrictions allows you to block types of apps, and restrict content according to age. You can also see what device they are using as well as add some money for your child to spend in the store.

Web Activity

Click 'activity' to view the child's computer activity. Scroll down the list and you'll see web browsing activity.

At the top you'll see web searches and the keywords they've typed in. You can click these keywords to see what search results they found.

55

Underneath that, websites visited are listed along with the address so you can click them to check them out.

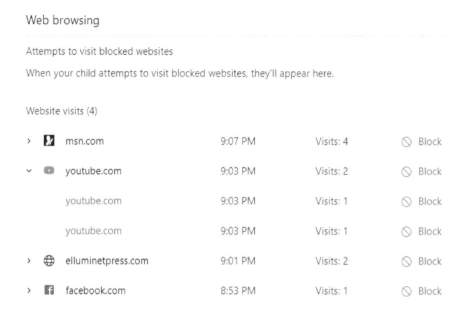

If you feel the site is inappropriate for your child to be looking at, click 'block' next to the website in the list.

Any attempts to visit blocked sites will appear at the top of this section.

If you want to allow your child to use the website again click 'allow'.

If you don't see any activity go to this website on their device, make sure you have verified the account on the device. Check out page 45.

App Usage

Click 'activity' to view the child's computer activity. Scroll down the list and you'll see web browsing activity. Underneath the web activity you'll see 'apps and games'

Apps and games   Changing settings

Recently used (10)

>	Edge 1 device	16 min	Can't block
>	Candy Crush Soda Saga 1 device	21min	Block
>	Newcastle 1 device	1 min	Block
>	Windows Maps 1 device	1 min	Block
>	Windows Store 1 device	1 min	Block
>	Facebook 1 device	< 1 min	Block
>	Instagram 1 device	< 1 min	Block
>	Internet Explorer 1 device	< 1 min	Block
>	Windows Calculator 1 device	< 1 min	Block

At the bottom of the page, you'll see a summary chart of the screen time spend on the computer for each day.

Screen time (122 min)   Set allowed times

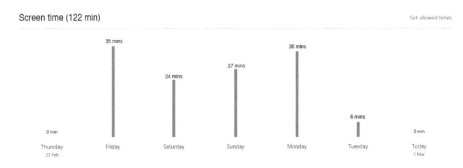

57

Screen Time & Curfews

You can set curfews and limits to the amount of time your children can use their devices. To do this click 'screen time'.

Screen time allows you to set curfews so you can prevent your children using their tablets or computers except in the designated hours.

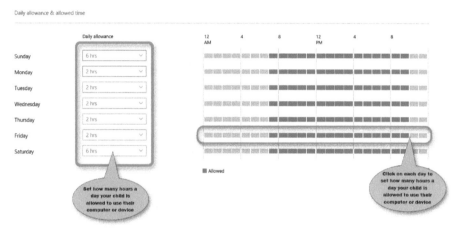

For example, you could set a time limit so your child can only use their tablet or computer between certain times of the day. Click on each day.

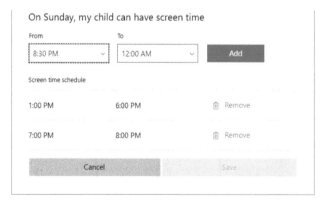

In the dialog box that appears, enter the times using the 'from' and 'to' fields. Click 'add' to add the times.

Set Up a Microsoft Account

You can sign up online by launching your web browser and going to the following address

```
signup.live.com
```

Fill in the form with your details. Choose a username. Microsoft will check to see if the username is available, if it's not available, you'll need to choose a different name - this will form the first half of your Microsoft Account email address.

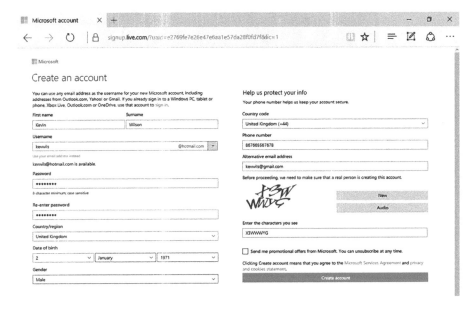

Enter the rest of your details, don't leave any fields blank.

At the bottom, you'll see what is known as a captcha. This is to make sure that only 'real people' create accounts and not automated bots. All you need to do, is in the field underneath, enter the characters that you see in the captcha image.

If you can't read them click 'new' to generate a new one, or click 'audio' and you'll hear an automated voice speak out the characters. Type what you hear into the field.

Un-tick 'send me promotional offers...'

Scroll down and click 'create account' at the bottom of the page.

Set up OneDrive

OneDrive comes with Windows 10 and is probably the safest place to store all your files as they are backed up in case your PC crashes.

If you signed into Windows 10 with your Microsoft Account, then OneDrive is usually installed.

To set it up, click the OneDrive's icon in the system tray on the bottom right hand side of the screen.

Enter your Microsoft Account email address then click 'sign in'.

Enter your password, then click 'sign in'.

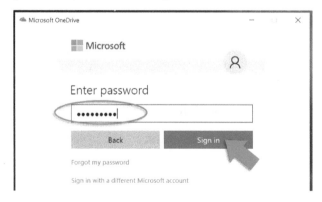

OneDrive will ask you where you want to store your OneDrive files on your computer while you work on them. Most of the time you can just leave it in it's default location. Click next.

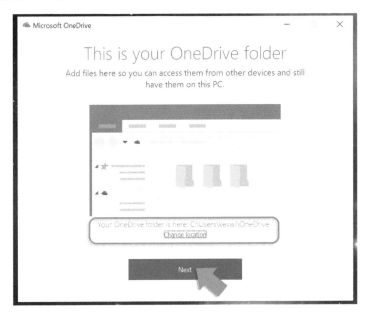

OneDrive will scan for directories and files on your OneDrive account and synchronise them with your local machine.

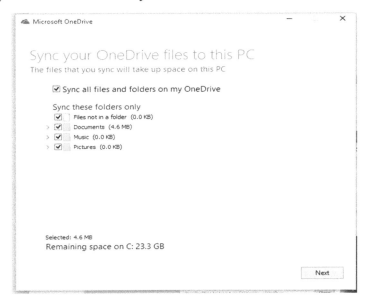

I usually select all of them. Click 'next'.

Chapter 2: Setting up Windows 10

The theory is, you work on the files on your local machine - you edit, update, create, save, and do the things you need to do. OneDrive automatically copies these updates onto your OneDrive Account in the Cloud. This is called synchronisation.

This means you can access your files from any of your devices whether it is a tablet, phone, laptop, or on the web.

Using File Explorer, you can find all your files in your OneDrive folder listed down the left hand side, as shown below.

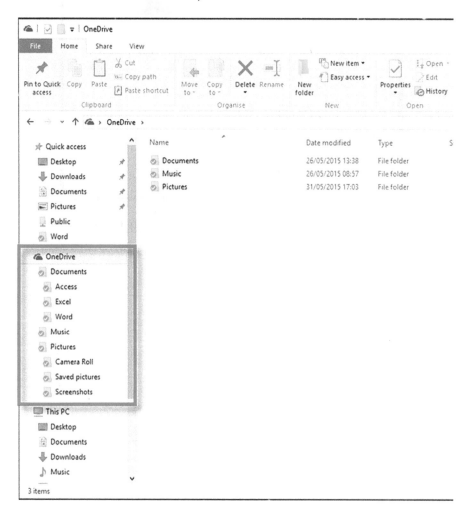

This is where you should save all your files you work on, in your apps.

Setting up Printers

The exact procedure to installing a printer differs from manufacturer to manufacturer. Each brand comes with its own menu style and software, however the general procedure is the same.

Downloading Printer Drivers

You'll need to install the printer software and drivers. You will need to go to the manufacturer's website to download the software.

For HP printers go to

> `support.hp.com/drivers`

For Canon printers go to

> `www.usa.canon.com/support`

For Brother printers go to

> `support.brother.com`

For Epson printers go to

> `www.epson.com/support`

Somewhere on the manufacturer's website, there will be a product search field. Type in the model name of your printer. In the example below, I'm installing an HP printer. In most cases you'll need to download the driver software from the manufacturer's website.

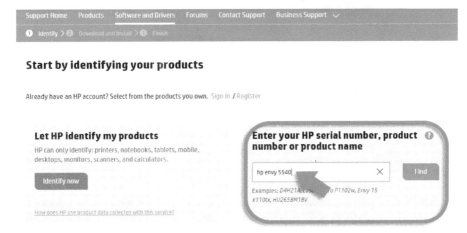

Click 'OK' or 'find'.

From the search results, select your Operating System if required, usually "Windows 10 (64bit)".

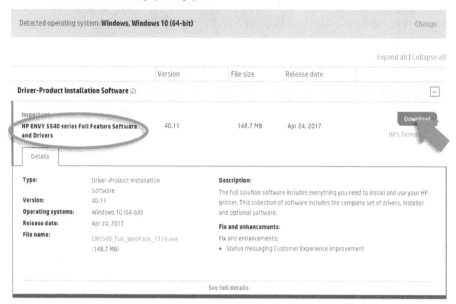

Click on the prompt at the bottom of your browser.

This will run the installation software. Click 'OK' or 'Yes' to the security prompt. If you don't see a prompt, go to your downloads folder in file explorer and double click on the EXE file you just downloaded. Follow the on screen instructions to connect to your printer.

Using USB

If you've downloaded the printer drivers as in the previous section, you won't need to do this bit.

Connect the printer to your computer using the USB cable.

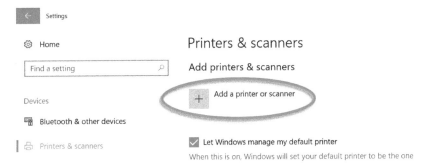

Open the Settings App from the Start menu.

Click 'devices'.

Click 'add a printer or scanner'.

Windows will detect most modern printers.

Using WiFi

If you've downloaded the printer drivers as in the previous section, you won't need to do this bit.

Most modern printers will detect your WiFi network and initiate a set up wizard on the LCD panel on the printer when you turn it on. This is definitely the way you'd want to connect to a printer if you are on a tablet or laptop.

On the printer's LCD panel, locate the network or wireless set up. The exact specifics on how to do this will depend on your printer, so you will need to refer to the set up instructions that came with the printer.

Select your Wi-Fi network and enter your network password.

Now on your computer/tablet, open the settings app from the Start menu.

Click 'devices' then 'add a printer or scanner'.

Windows will search for your printer.

Older Printers

If Windows doesn't detect your printer or you have an older printer, click 'the printer I want isn't listed.'

 Refresh

Searching for printers and scanners

The printer that I want isn't listed

For printers connected via USB select 'my printer is a little older, help me find it.'

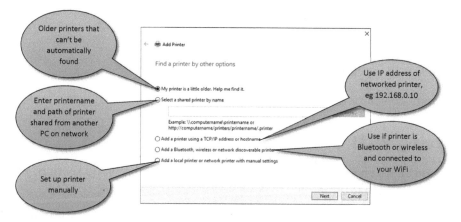

Select your printer from the results list, click 'next', then give the printer a name if required, click 'next'.

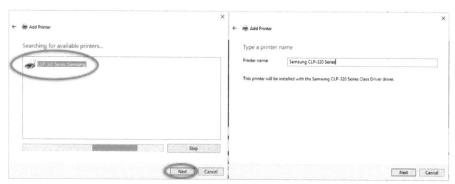

Select 'do not share this printer' then click next.

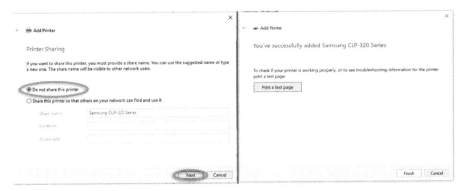

Once you're done, click 'finish'.

Managing Printers

You can get to the print queue from the Settings App. From the Settings App, click 'devices'.

On the left hand side of the window, click 'printers & scanners', then select your printer. From the options that open up, click 'open queue'.

This will open up the print queue for that printer.

Here you can see a list of documents that are queued for printing. If you right click on the print job in the list, you can cancel or pause the document.

You can also change global printer settings and preferences here too.

Setting up Windows Hello

Windows Hello is Microsoft's new biometric security feature built into some Windows 10 devices. Not all tablets and PCs support this, however this is likely to change as the technology develops.

Windows Hello allows you to sign into your device and certain services and websites, using a finger print or face scan instead of a password. You will need a compatible web cam or finger print scanner on your device/PC to do this.

Currently the only devices that support this feature are

- Surface Books

- Surface Pro Tablets

- Some Lumia Phones

- Any PC or Laptop with a 'RealSense' camera or a finger print scanner

Windows Hello gives you some extra sign in options. Tap your settings icon, then choose Accounts. From Accounts tap 'sign in options'

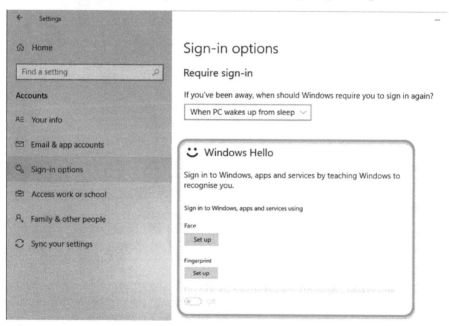

Under Windows Hello, choose the sign in option you want to use: face recognition or fingerprint.

Finger Print Scanner

Select 'set up' under the fingerprint section of the 'sign in' options in the settings app.

Scroll down to the windows hello section and click 'set up' under 'fingerprint'.

Scan your finger using the fingerprint reader. Most people use their index finger You may need to do this a few times. Keep going until Windows informs you the process is complete.

Select close.

You should now be able to sign in with your fingerprint from the lock screen. You might have to tap 'sign in options' if the feature isn't automatically selected.

So instead of typing in a password, I can now just swipe my finger on the scanner to sign into my account.

Facial Recognition

To use this feature you will however need a webcam that supports this technology. Something like the "windows hello camera", shown below.

If you have a Microsoft device such as a surface studio, surface tablet or surface book, the web cam is built in.

Tap your settings icon, then choose 'accounts'. From the accounts page, tap 'sign in options'

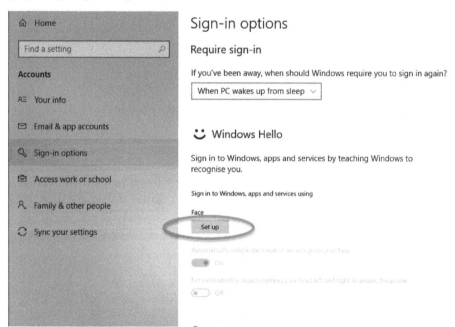

Under 'face' select 'set up'.

On your screen you'll see an image from your webcam. Make sur can see your whole face and head in the image. Keep looking at screen, until Windows has completed the scan. It will usually take few seconds.

Windows Hello setup   ✕

Keep looking directly at your screen.

Cancel

Make sure you turn on 'automatically unlock the screen if we recognise your face'.

Close the settings app.

Now when you turn on your computer, you won't need to sign in with a password, you just look at your screen and Windows will unlock your account for you.

Navigating Windows 10

In this chapter we will take a look at the features of Windows 10, how to get the most out of them and how to use these features to get your work done.

We'll start with some navigational features that allow you to start apps and interact with Windows.

Lets begin by looking at the start menu.

Start Menu

The start menu, in Spring Creator's Update, has had a few minor enhancements.

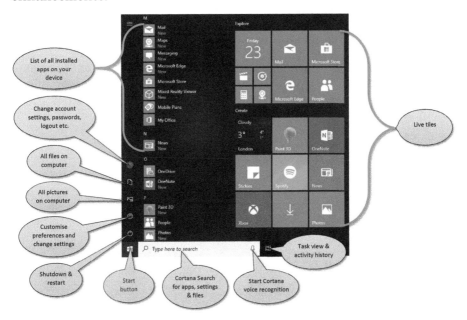

Listed down the far left hand side of your menu you'll see five little icons. From top to bottom, these icons allow you to change your account password or log out, view all files & pictures using file explorer, system settings, and shut down.

Also down the left is a list of your most frequently used applications. Underneath this list is an alphabetical list of all apps installed on your system.

On the right hand side of the menu, you'll see coloured tiles representing apps. This is the tile area and these tiles are sometimes called live tiles. Live tiles graphically represent apps and can also display basic notifications such as latest messages, or emails from your mail app, information such as weather, latest news headlines and so on, even when the app isn't running. To run the app you just click on the tile.

The start menu can be displayed as a menu on the bottom left hand side of the screen. This is better suited to point and click users, and is called desktop mode. The start menu can also fill the whole screen, putting more emphasis on the application tiles on the right hand side. This is called tablet mode and is useful for touch screen users using tablets and smartphones.

Tile Folders

Windows 10 allows you to group tiles into folders. This can be useful if you have a lot of apps installed on your device. You can start to group your tiles into logical folders; meaning you can group all your communication apps such as facebook, browser, or email, into one folder; all your office apps into another folder and so on.

In this example, I am going to drag all my communication apps into one folder - email, edge, facebook and twitter apps. So choose one of the apps to be the folder: edge browser. Then drag the other apps: email, facebook and twitter to this app, as illustrated below.

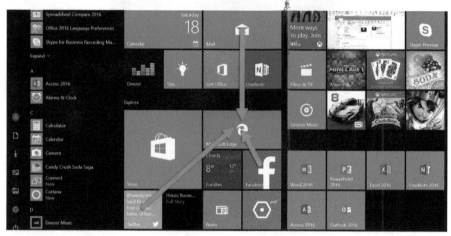

Now all these apps will be grouped into a folder, shown below left. Clicking on the folder will open up your app tiles, shown below right.

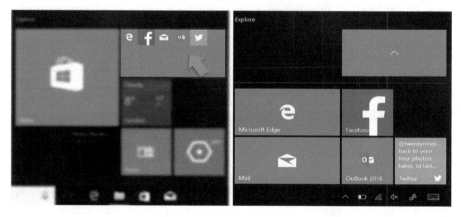

Customising your Start Menu

It is a good idea to customise Windows 10's start menu to your personal preferences and needs. We can do this by arranging, adding and removing tiles on the menu. *quantam mechanks*

Add Tiles to Start Menu

You can add tiles by dragging the icon off the list of apps on the left hand side of the start menu, to the tile section as shown below.

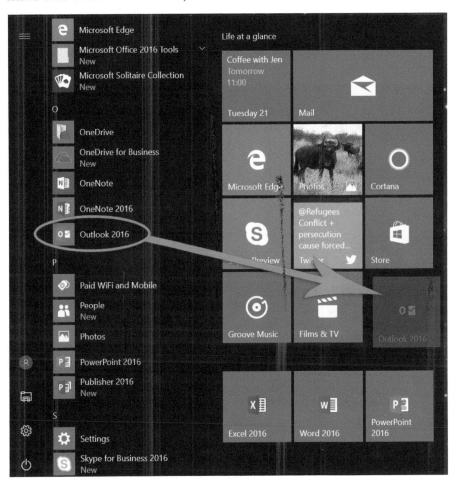

In this way, you can build up a start menu where you can easily access all the apps you use the most, without having to scroll through lists of apps on your start menu.

This is particularly useful if you happen to have a lot of apps installed on your machine.

By doing this, I have built up the following start menu, and created tiles for the apps I use the most by dragging them from the list of apps on the left hand side, into position on the tile area.

This way, you can maximise the use of your machine by removing tiles you don't use or need, keeping and adding tiles for the apps you use the most and grouping them into sections. You can see below, all my Adobe apps are together, and underneath, all my Microsoft Office apps.

Also I have access to my calendar; I like to keep up with the news, so I've added the news app; as well as the local weather forecasts, which I find useful.

If the app you want to add to your start menu isn't listed, you can search for it using the search field on your start menu.

In this example I want to add the app called 'wordpad' to the start menu.

I can search for it using the search field. When windows finds the app, it will list it under a heading called 'Apps'.

Right click on the app icon and from the menu that appears select 'pin to start'.

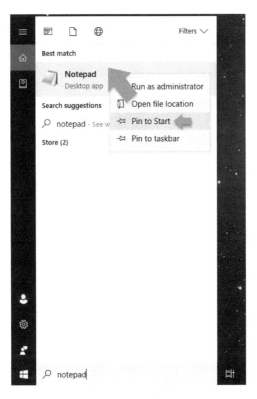

Here you can see, the icon has been pinned as a tile on the start menu. You may have to drag the tile into position.

Move Tiles on the Start Menu

You can move tiles by clicking and dragging them to a new position. The tiles will scroll automatically as you drag your tile up and down the menu.

In the example below, I want to put Outlook 2016 with the rest of the Office 2016 Apps on my start menu. To do this, just click Outlook 2016 icon, and drag it down to the position where the rest of the Office Apps are.

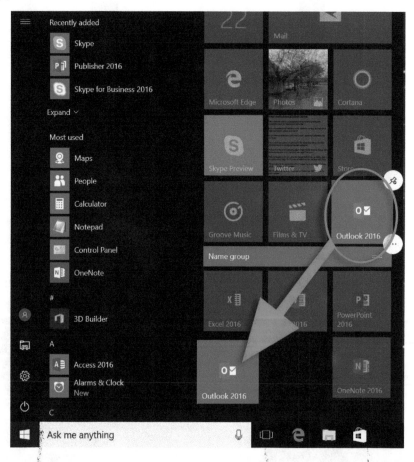

If you are on a touch screen device, tap and hold your finger on the tile for a second, then drag your finger down the screen to the position you want your tile.

Arranging and grouping your tiles like this helps to keep everything organised and easy to find.

Remove Tiles from Start Menu

To remove a tile, right click on it and select the 'unpin icon' that appears on the top right of the tile.

If you are on a touch screen device, tap and hold your finger on the tile until the icons appear.

Windows 10 has a habit of adding tiles you don't use, so it's a good idea to remove all the tiles you don't use, to prevent things from getting too confusing or cluttered.

This will also give you more space to add tiles for the Apps you use all the time, making them more accessible and easy to find.

Resize Tiles on Start Menu

To resize a tile, right click on it. If you are on a touch screen device, tap and hold your finger on the icon to get the icons to appear.

From the two little icons that appear, click the one with the three dots, then from the menu that appears, click resize.

From the slide out menu, click the size you want. You will see that each tile as a number of pre-set sizes.

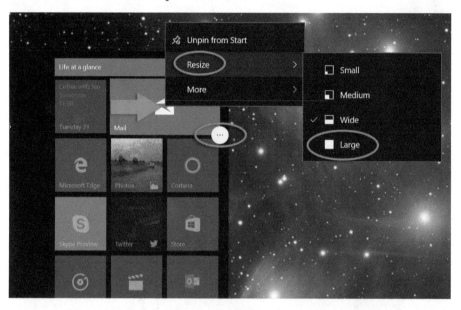

There are usually four sizes to choose from. Small, medium, wide and large. You can see the differences below.

Some app tiles may not have all the sizes available.

Pin Icons to your TaskBar

For more convenience, you can pin all your favourite apps to your task bar along the bottom of your screen.

To do this, right click on the app in the list on the left hand side or on a live tile. Click the icon with the three dots. From the menu that appears, select 'more'.

From the slide out menu select 'pin to taskbar'

You'll see the icon has been added to your taskbar. If you right click on the icon on your taskbar, you can see a list of recently opened files. Click the little pin icon on the right hand side of the file name to pin the file to the list permanently, if you use that file all the time.

File Explorer

File explorer can be used to find your files on your computer, access your OneDrive, network resources and external hard drives or flash drives. You can find it on your taskbar or on your start menu.

Down the left hand side you will find a list of all the libraries of files on your computer, ie documents, photographs, music and videos.

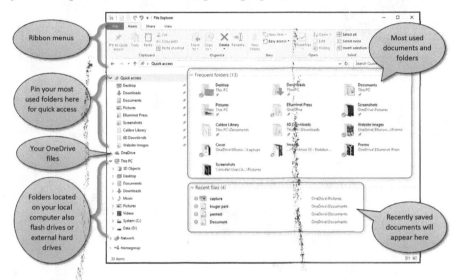

At the top, Windows will start to list the most used libraries you have accessed.

If you click on 'quick access' you will see a list of your most recently accessed files.

Along the top of the explorer window you will see the ribbon menus. Much like the style introduced in Microsoft Office, tools and features are grouped into ribbons.

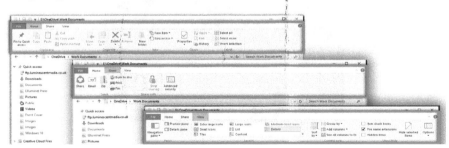

Home Ribbon

On the home ribbon, you'll find all your most common tools, such as copy and paste files, create folders, move files, delete files and show file properties.

Share Ribbon

On the share ribbon you can burn files to a CD, print them, zip them up into a compressed file - useful if you want to email a few documents together. Or you can share files with other computers on your home network or home group if you have one set up.

View Ribbon

With the view ribbon you can display your files as a list, as icons and as thumbnails. Icons and thumbnail views can be useful for browsing photographs.

Do this by clicking on the layout options in the middle of the ribbon (large icons, medium sized icons, list or details).

You can also sort files by date added, alphabetically or by size.

Do this by clicking 'sort by'. From the menu, select 'name' to list your files alphabetically by name, or click 'date...' to sort by 'date edited' or 'date created'.

Sharing Files from File Explorer

Share option on right click context menu. Right click on the file you want to share, then from the popup menu, select 'share'.

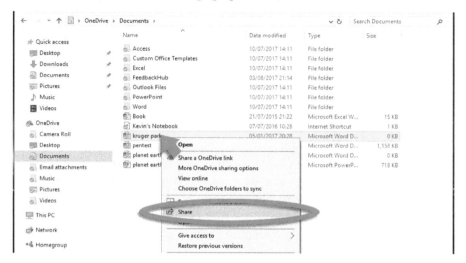

From the popup dialog box, select the person you want to share the document with. Contacts that you have added to the people app or pinned to your taskbar will appear at the top. If the contact is not in the list, you can send via email or skype at the bottom.

The options will depend on what apps you have installed.

In this example, I am going to email the document. An integrated email will appear in the window allowing you to type a message.

Click 'send' when you're ready to send your email.

Near Share

Allows you to share files between devices in the same vicinity using Bluetooth. First you'll need to turn on near share. To do this, open up your action center. You'll see an icon called 'nearby sharing'. Click this to turn it on.

In file explorer right-click the file you want to share. Select 'share' from the popup menu.

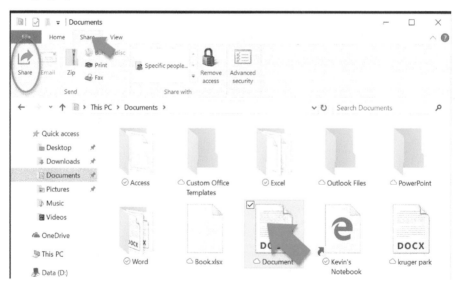

You can also share from Edge and most other apps using the share icon

In the share dialog box, you'll see a list of devices in the near vicinity. Click on the device you want to share the file with.

In this example, I am sharing a document from my laptop to a surface tablet. The surface tablet is named ORION.

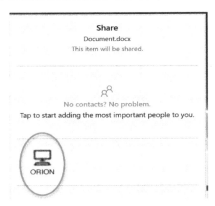

If you're having trouble finding other devices, go to the settings app, select 'system', then 'shared experiences' and under 'nearby sharing', change 'I can share or receive content from' to 'everyone nearby'. Do this on both devices.

On the other device, a notification will appear in Action Center asking for confirmation.

Click 'open' to receive the document. All your received files will be stored in your downloads folder.

Basic File Management

There are many different types of file types; files for photos, videos, documents, speadsheets, presentations and so on. These files are identified by a file extension.

`filename.extension`

So for example...

A photograph is usually saved as a JPEG or JPG. Eg **photo-of-sophie.jpg**. This could be from a graphics package or a camera.

A document is usually saved as a DOC or DOCX. Eg: **production-resume.docx**. This is usually from a word processor such as Microsoft Word.

The 3 or 4 letters after the period is called a file extension and it is what Windows uses to identify the application needed to open the file.

It's best to save all your files into your OneDrive.

Windows stores your files in a hierarchical tree like structure.

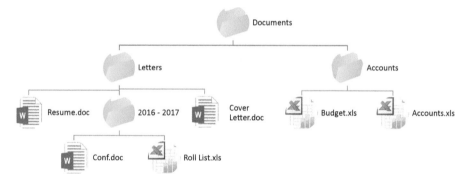

You can create yellow folders to store files of the same type or for the same purpose.

In the example above, letters to various recipients are stored in a 'letters' folder. Similarly, all files to do with the accounts are stored in an 'accounts' folder.

Storing files in this fashion keeps them organised and makes them easier to find.

Creating Folders

It's a good idea to create folders to help organise all your files. You could have a folder for your personal documents, work documents, presentations, vacation/holiday photos, college work and so on. To do this open your File Explorer.

On the left hand side of your screen, navigate to the place you want to create a folder. In this example, I'm going to create a folder in my 'OneDrive'.

From the home ribbon along the top of your screen, click 'new folder'.

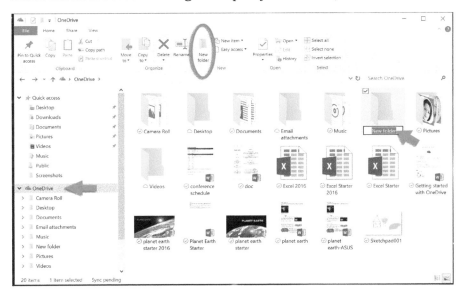

On the right hand side of your screen, you'll see a new folder appear called 'new folder'.

Delete the text 'new folder' and type in a meaningful name - ideally the name of the group of documents you are saving into this folder.

Moving Files

There are a few methods to use when moving or copying files. I prefer the drag and drop method - which seems quicker and easier.

Open your File Explorer

On the left hand side of the window, open up the folder you want to move your file into. In the example below, I am going to move some excel documents into my 'excel' folder. My 'excel' folder is in my 'documents' folder on OneDrive.

So I'm going to click on OneDrive, go down to 'documents' and click on the small down arrow on the left hand side to open the folder. Inside here, you can see the 'excel' folder in the 'documents' folder.

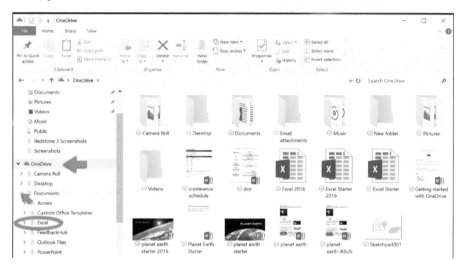

Now click on the folder where the document you want to move is saved. In this example, the file is saved in OneDrive and is called 'excel 2016'. All you need to do is drag and drop the file into the folder, as shown below.

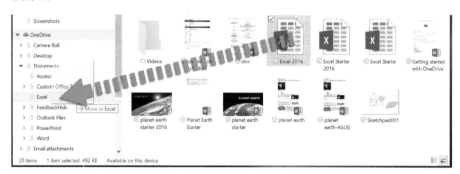

Copying Files

Open your File Explorer

On the left hand side of the window, open up the folder you want to copy your file into. In the example below, I am going to copy an excel document into my excel folder. My excel folder is in my documents folder on OneDrive.

So I'm going to click on OneDrive, go down to 'documents' and click on the small down arrow on the left hand side to open the folder. Inside here, you can see the 'excel' folder in the 'documents' folder.

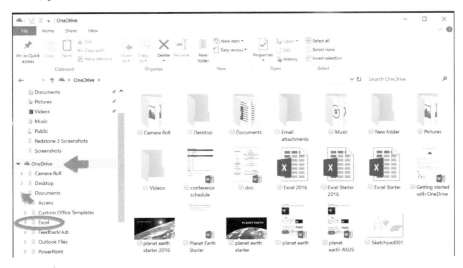

Now click on the folder where the document you want to copy is saved. In this example, the file is saved in OneDrive and is called 'excel Starter 2016'.

All you need to do is hold down the control key (ctrl), then drag and drop the file into the folder, as shown below.

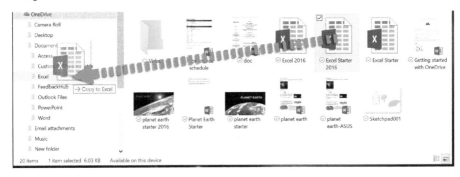

Renaming Files

To rename a file, open up your File Explorer and find the file you want to rename.

Navigate to the folder your file is saved in. In this demo it's in the OneDrive, Documents folder. Click on the file to select it.

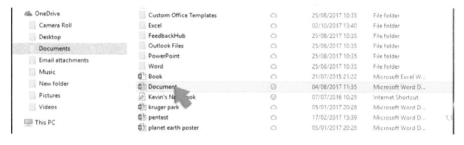

From the home ribbon click 'rename'.

You'll see the name of the file highlighted in blue.

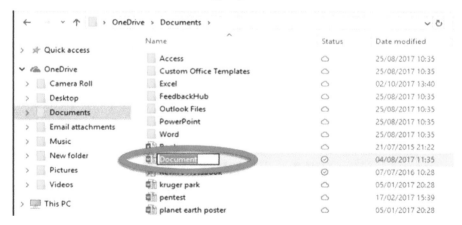

Now type the new name of the file.

External Drives

You can attach storage devices to your computer. The most common ones are memory sticks; also called usb keys, usb sticks, flash drives or thumb drives. The other types are portable hard drives.

Memory sticks are usually smaller in capacity ranging from 1GB all the way up to 256GB. Portable hard drives can be larger than 1TB.

When you plug one of these devices into your computer, the device will show up in File Explorer, under the 'This PC' section.

Double click the drive icon, circled above, to open the contents of the drive.

OneDrive

OneDrive is your cloud file hosting service and synchronises your files between your device (pc, laptop, phone or tablet), and the cloud file hosting service.

You'll find OneDrive in your File Explorer window. OneDrive is where you should save all your files from Microsoft Office, photographs, music, videos and so on. The advantage is, if your computer crashes, you won't lose all your files as they will still be stored on OneDrive.

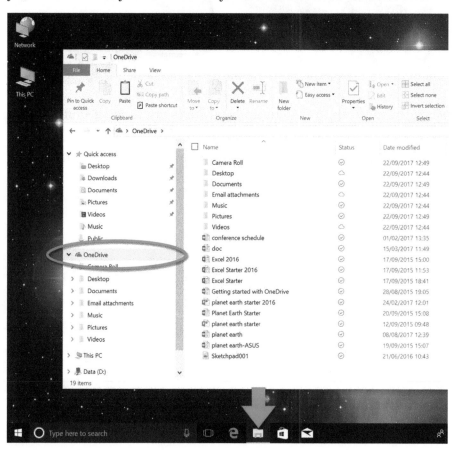

The other advantage of OneDrive, is you can access all your files on all your devices. So you can see your documents on your PC, phone, tablet or laptop, and you can access them from anywhere that has an internet connection.

Files on Demand

Files On-Demand stores all your files on OneDrive Cloud and allows you to open them from Windows File Explorer.

Once you open your file, it is then downloaded to your device. This works with devices that have limited local storage such as tablets and smart phones, that do not have enough space to hold your entire OneDrive contents.

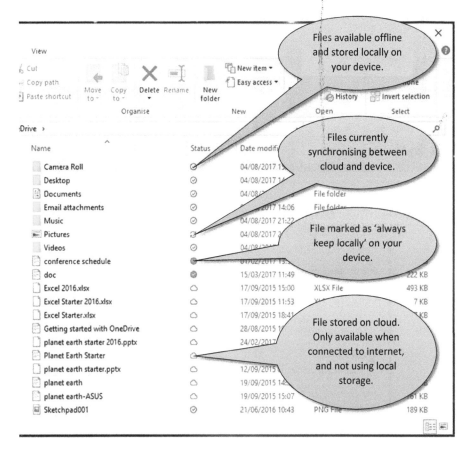

One the icons themselves or in the status column, you'll see some status indicators - as you can see in the illustration above.

Enable and Disable Files On Demand

Right-click the OneDrive cloud icon in the notification area. From the popup menu select 'settings'.

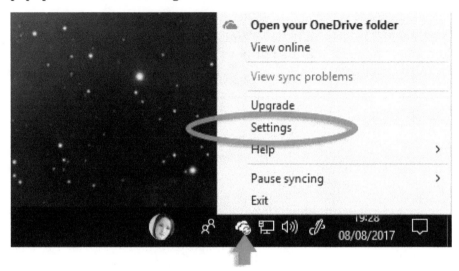

Select the 'settings' tab.

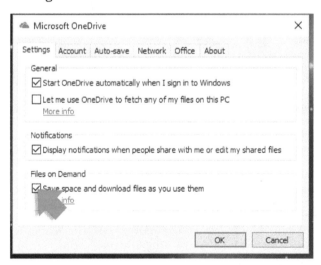

Under 'Files On-Demand', click the tick box next to 'Save space and download files as you use them' to enable the feature.

This will mark all your files as 'online', meaning they are stored on OneDrive Cloud not on your device. When you select a file to open, your file is downloaded to your device and then opened.

Making files available Offline

Having full access to all your files on OneDrive without having do download the whole contents to your device is great, but what happens if you don't always have an internet connection? Well, you can mark certain files as 'available offline', meaning OneDrive will download these files to your device.

To do this, select the files you want to make available offline - hold down control and select your files, if you want more than one.

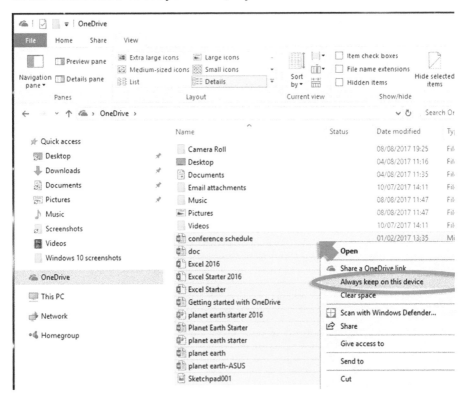

Right click on the selected files and from the popup menu select, 'always keep on this device'.

OneDrive will download the selected files to your device so you can access them when you don't have a connection. If you change your files while offline, OneDrive will sync the changes once you connect to the internet.

Task Bar

The task bar has two new options, one is the Cortana/Windows search box. This allows you to search for anything on your device or ask Cortana a question.

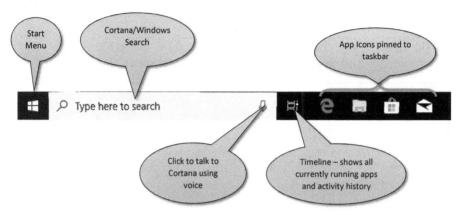

The other button is the timeline option that allows you to see currently running apps as well as your activity history. This enables you to switch to that app by tapping on its icon.

On the far right you will see the system tray. This has icons representing wifi networks, volume control, action center, as well as a clock and date. You can click on these to view their details. Eg, click on the clock/time to view your calendar and upcoming events, or click on the volume control to adjust your audio volume.

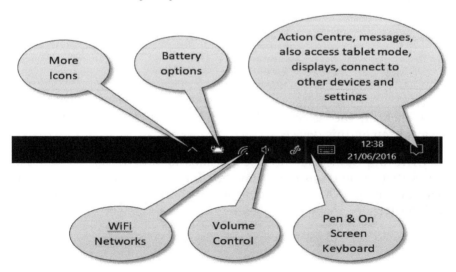

Action Centre

The action centre shows alerts and messages from different applications. You can find action centre by clicking the icon on the bottom right of the task bar, or swiping inwards from the right hand edge of your screen.

These notifications could be email message that have just arrived, system messages or status alerts from applications.

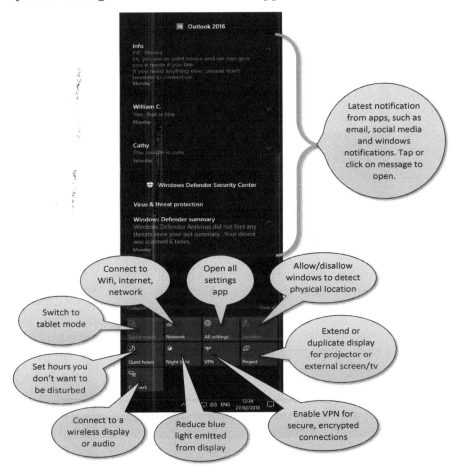

Along the bottom of the notifications window you will see some common settings, eg tablet mode, display settings, media connect for connecting to projectors, second screens etc.

Timeline Activity History

You'll find the timeline button on your task bar on the bottom left of your screen next to the Cortana search field.

Underneath you'll see a history of apps, websites and files you've used organised in reverse chronological order.

Files and apps you are currently running, will appear at the top. You can click or tap on these to switch to them.

Along the right hand side you'll see the timeline. You can drag this down to browse through your activity history. You'll see apps and files you've had open listed according to the date you last used them. Click or tap on any of these files to go back to where you left off.

On the top right you'll see a magnifying glass.

This allows you to search for activities, files you've used and so on.

Using Multiple Desktops

'Multiple desktops' is almost like having two or more desks in your office where you can do your work. You could have a desktop for your web browsing and email, another desktop for your word processing, another desktop for your photo editing and sharing and so on.

Multiple desktops help to organise your tasks together. So you can keep things you are working on together.

Click on 'new desktop' to open a new desktop, then you can open the apps you want to run.

In this example, open Word and Edge. Click the timeline button on the task bar, then click 'new desktop'. Now open Email and Calendar. Hit the task view button again and click 'new desktop'. Now open Groove Music and TV & Videos app.

So now I have a desktop for my word processing and internet research with Microsoft Word and Edge Browser, a second desktop for email & calendar, and a third desktop for entertainment with Groove Music and TV.

To switch between the desktops, click on the thumbnails listed across the top of the screen (Desktop 1, Desktop 2, Desktop 3 and so on). You'll see it's easier to flick between the apps when they are grouped into different desktops for similar tasks and projects. This is like having a different desk in your office for each project you're working on.

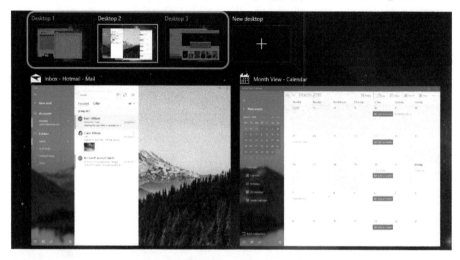

To get a preview of what is running on a particular desktop, hover your mouse over the thumbnails listed across the top of the screen. You will see previews of the apps running underneath. To switch to an app click on its thumbnail.

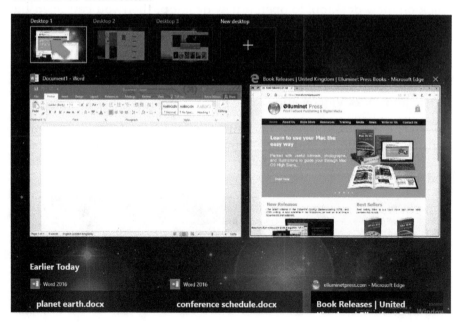

Multiple Screens

You can plug in more than one screen into most modern computers or tablets if you have the correct adapters.

You can set up multiple screens by right clicking on your desktop and selecting 'display settings'.

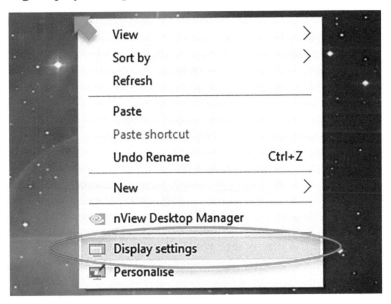

Select 'extend these displays' from the 'multiple displays' drop down menu shown below.

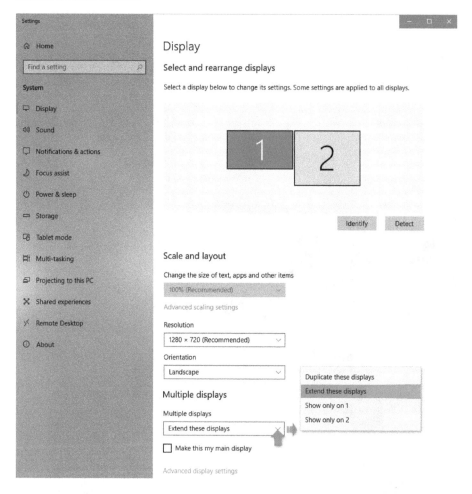

Your screens are identified by a number, shown above. To check which is which, click 'identify' and you'll see a big number appear on each screen.

Make sure you click on your main display using the numbered rectangular icons at the top of the screen. Remembering which number appeared on which screen, click the one you use to do most of your work and click 'make this my main display'. This tells apps that this 'main display' is the one where you will control windows from and do most of your work.

The other display becomes your secondary display; a second desk. This could be another monitor, tv screen or projector.

Using Projectors

Much like using multiple screens, you can also use a projector as your second display.

Open your action center; click the icon on the bottom right of your taskbar.

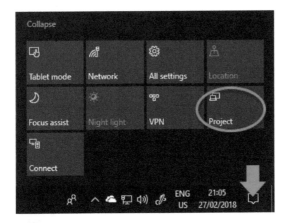

You can also press Windows-P on your keyboard. From the options, select the display you want.

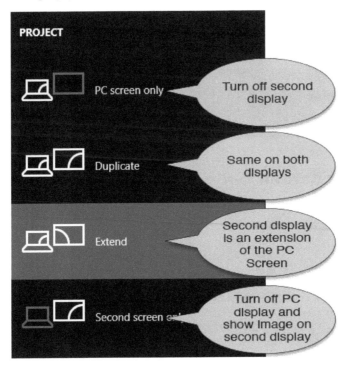

<u>Duplicate</u> PC screen onto Second Screen

Everything you do on the laptop screen (PC Screen) will be duplicated on the second screen (eg projector). So both screens will show the same image.

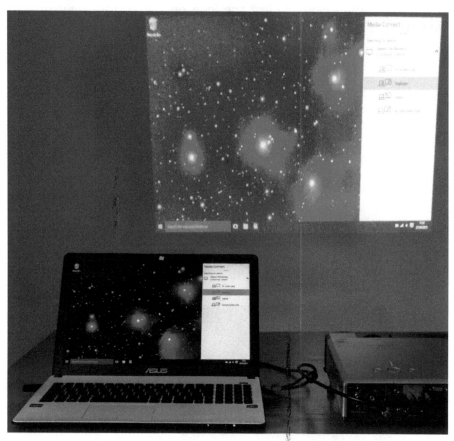

Second Screen Only

This disables your PC's monitor and allows the display to only appear on the second screen.

PC Screen Only

This disables the projector and allows the information to be seen only on the PC's monitor.

Extend PC screen onto Second Screen

The second screen (such as a projector) acts as an extension to your laptop screen (PC Screen), rather than just a duplicate. So you can have something on your laptop screen and show different images on the projector as shown below.

This allows you to move windows from the laptop's screen (PC Screen 1) to Screen 2 (eg projector) and vice versa.

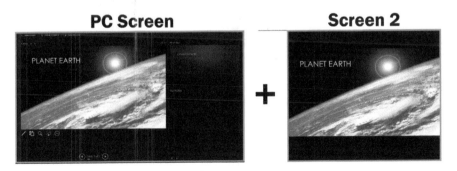

Screen 2 becomes an extension of the PC Screen. Ideal for using software presentation software such as Pro Presenter or PowerPoint.

Using Continuum

Windows 10 is designed to run seamlessly on all your devices. Whether you are using a phone, tablet, xbox, laptop/notebook or desktop PC, Windows 10 will automatically select the correct mode for your phone or tablet with a touch screen interface or a desktop/laptop PC with a point and click interface.

Desktop PC/Laptop

Windows 10 is capable of running on a full sized desktop computer or workstation and runs in a similar way to Windows 7 did back in its day, with mouse, keyboard and the start menu available to access your files and programs. This is desktop mode.

Tablets

Tablet mode is tailored to smaller screens and touch interfaces. So instead of a keyboard and mouse, you tap on the icons on the screen with your finger. To make this easer, icons are larger and apps run full screen.

For convertible devices, such as the Surface, there are two modes, tablet and desktop.

When using the device as a tablet, Windows 10 will automatically change to tablet mode which is more touch-friendly.

Once you connect a mouse and keyboard, or flip your laptop around, Windows will go into desktop mode. Apps turn back into desktop windows that are easier to move around with a mouse and you'll see your desktop again.

For Phones

Another new feature of Continuum is the ability to use your phone as if it were a PC. However, this only works on Lumia phones and requires a purchase of a display dock. You will need to connect a keyboard, mouse and monitor to the dock.

Just plug your phone into the dock and you can use your apps as if you were using your PC or connect to projectors to present. This way you always have your files with you.

109

Linking your Phone

You can link to any smartphone such as an iPhone, Android or Windows Phone.

From the Settings App, select Phone. Click on 'add a phone'.

Enter your phone number and click 'send'. This will send a message to your phone. Your phone will now be linked and will show up in the 'your phone' section of the settings app.

Manage phones

ElluminetPress
iOS

Add a phone

Manage all devices linked with your Microsoft account

Unlink this PC

If you unlink this PC, it will no longer be able to receive tasks and documents you've sent from your phone.

On your phone, go to the app store, open the search and type

```
Continue on PC
```

Tap 'get' or 'download' to download the app to your phone.

The first time you use this feature, you'll need to enable it. To do this open an app such as Safari and tap the share icon.

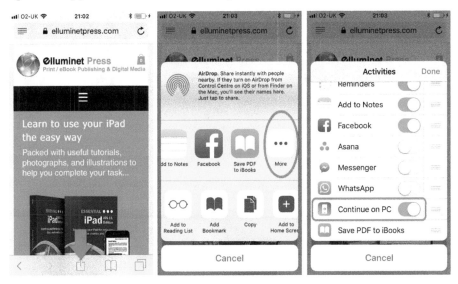

Scroll across the top section and tap the 'more' icon. Scroll down the list of activities until you see 'continue on PC'. Set the slider to green to turn it on. Tap 'done'.

Now to share something, tap the share icon in your app and select 'continue on PC'

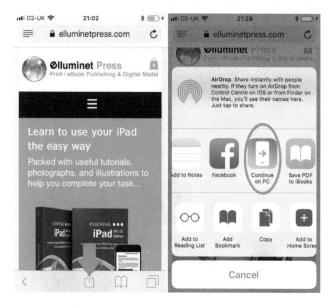

If this is the first time you've used this feature, you'll need to sign in with your Microsoft Account email address and password.

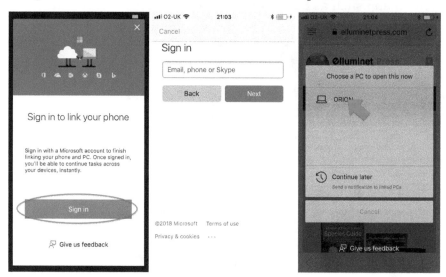

Select the device you want to share the page with.

You can do this with most apps on your phone that have the sharing feature. Not all apps will support this feature.

Arranging Windows on Desktop

It's useful when working in Windows 10 to arrange the windows on your desktop, especially when you're using more than one application at a time. For example, you could be browsing the web and writing a Word document at the same time- perhaps you're researching something, you could have Word open and your web browser next to it on the screen.

Lets take a look at moving and resizing widows on the desktop.

Moving a Window

Move your mouse pointer to the top of the window.

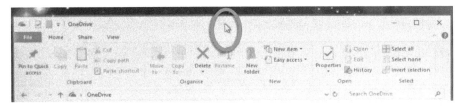

Now click and drag the window to your desired position on the screen.

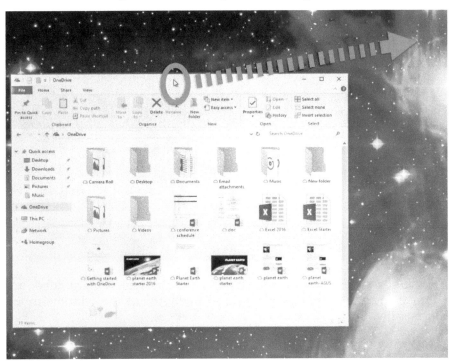

Resizing a Window

To resize a window, move your mouse pointer to the bottom right corner of the window - your pointer should turn into a double edged arrow.

The double edged arrow means you can resize the window. Now click and drag the edge of the window until it is the size you want.

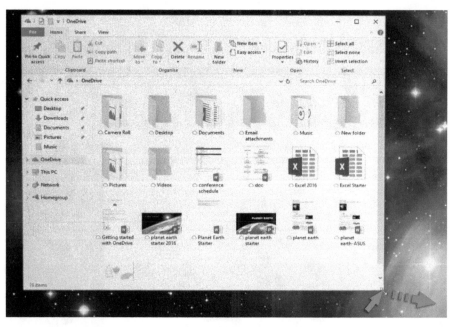

You can drag any edge of the window - left, bottom or right edge, but I find using the corner allows you to freely resize the window much more easily.

If you're on a touch screen, tap and drag the corner of the window.

Minimise, Maximise & Close a Window

On the top right hand side of every window, you'll see three icons. You can use these icons to minimise a window, ie reduce it to the taskbar essentially hiding the window from the desktop. With the second icon, you can maximise the window so it fills the entire screen, or if the window is already maximised, using the same icon, restore the window to its original size, and the third icon you can use to close a window completely.

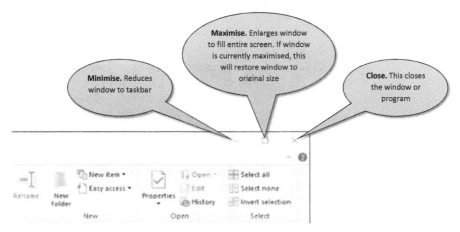

Using Windows Side by Side

Using the move and resize window skills covered earlier, you can arrange your windows on your desktop.

Window Snap Feature

You can now have four apps snapped on the same screen with a new quadrant layout.

Windows will also show other apps and programs running for additional snapping and even make smart suggestions on filling available screen space with other open apps.

Click and drag the window to the right edge of the screen until your mouse pointer is on the edge and you see a translucent box appear on the right hand half of the screen.

Keyboard Shortcuts

Keyboard shortcuts are performed using 3 main function keys: the control key, the windows key and the alt key.

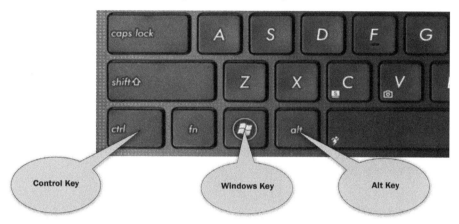

To execute a command using a keyboard shortcut. Hold down the appropriate function key and tap the key for the function you want shown in the table below.

Windows + Tab	Opens thumbnail list of open applications
Windows + A	Open Windows 10 notification centre
Windows + D	Show Windows desktop
Windows + E	Open Windows Explorer
Windows + K	Connect to wireless displays and audio devices
Windows + P	Project a screen
Windows + R	Run a command
Windows + X	Open Start button context menu
Windows key + Arrow key	Snap app windows left, right, corners, maximize, or minimize
Windows key + Comma	Temporarily peek at the desktop
Windows Key	Show windows start menu
Alt + Tab	Switch to previous window
Alt + Space	Reveals drop down menu on current window: Restore, move, size, minimize, maximize or close.
Alt + F4	Close current app
Ctrl + Shift + Esc	Open Task Manager
Ctrl + Z	Undo Command
Ctrl + X	Cut selected text
Ctrl + C	Copy selected text
Ctrl + V	Paste selected text at cursor position
Ctrl + P	Print

Other Features

Other features worth noting are the Dynamic Lock, Storage Sense, Blue Light Reduction and App Throttling.

Dynamic Lock

Before activating the dynamic lock, you will first need to pair your device or phone with your PC or laptop via Bluetooth. To activate dynamic lock go to...

Settings App -> Accounts -> Sign-in Options -> Dynamic Lock

Tick the box next to 'Allow Windows to detect when you're away and automatically lock the device.'

Storage Sense

Over time, temporary files, caches and files in the recycle bin start to accumulate. Storage sense monitors and deletes these files, keeping your system running smoothly. This feature is disabled by default but you can enable it easily from the Settings App.

Settings App -> System -> Storage -> Storage Sense

Switch the slider to 'on'.

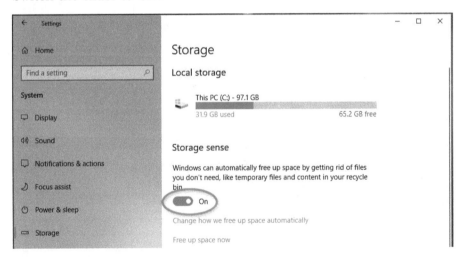

Click 'clean up space now' to manually run the clean-up.

Click 'change how we free up space automatically'.

Set 'run storage sense' to 'when windows decides'. This will allow Windows to automatically manage disk space by deleting cached and temporary files as and when it needs to.

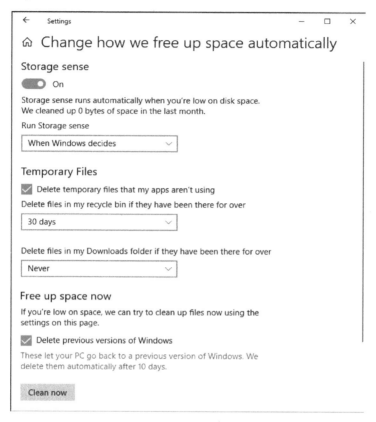

Under the 'temporary files' section, set 'delete files in my recycle bin...' to '30 days'. I don't usually allow Windows to delete files in my downloads folder, as sometimes I like to reuse or keep things I have downloaded from the web. However if you don't do this, then you can allow Windows to delete files in your downloads folder after a certain number of days - usually 30 days is a good setting.

At the bottom, select 'delete previous versions of Windows'. This allows Windows 10 to remove backup files it saved of your previous installation of Windows. This could be Windows 7 or 8, or an earlier version of Windows 10. It is safe to delete these files. They're only required if you plan to remove Windows 10 and go back an earlier version.

Once you're done, hit 'clean now'. Windows will automatically clear temporary files and empty the recycle bin during its maintenance schedule, so this feature can work silently in the background and you don't have to worry about it.

Blue Light Reduction

This feature is designed to reduce the amount of blue light emitted from your device's screen in the evenings, which is said to suppress the secretion of melatonin in the brain affecting your ability to sleep.

To turn it on, go to...

Settings App -> System -> Display

Under 'night light', switch the slider to 'on' then click 'night light settings'.

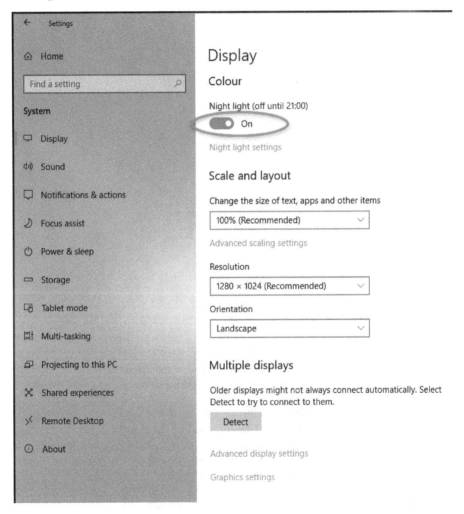

Click 'turn on now'. You can adjust the level of the night light using the 'colour temperature at night' slider.

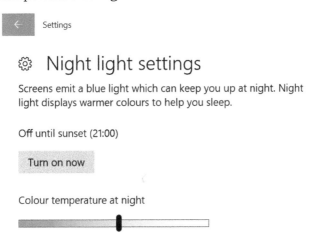

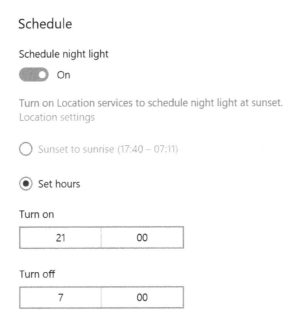

If you want the night light to come on at a specific time each night, shift the 'schedule night light' slider to 'on' and enter the time in the 'turn on' field and the time to turn it off in the 'turn off' field.

You'll see the screen turn an orange colour. Any work you produce, such as printing, editing, or photos, will not have the orange tint.

Pairing Devices with Bluetooth

On your Phone or device go to action centre and tap bluetooth, make sure it's turned on.

On your PC/Laptop go to

Settings App -> Devices -> Bluetooth

Shift the Bluetooth slider to 'on'. When you turn on your Bluetooth, your laptop or PC will start scanning for other Bluetooth devices such as your phone and list them in this window.

Click on the device you want to pair with and click 'pair', in this example the device is called 'WinPhone'. You'll see a randomly generated passcode pop up in a dialog box.

Type this code into the prompt on your phone and hit OK. Some devices won't need a passcode such as headphones, pens, mice and some keyboards.

Cortana Personal Assistant

Cortana is Microsoft's voice activated, personal assistant. You can use Cortana to set reminders using your natural voice rather than typing or clicking an icon.

You can ask Cortana questions about current weather and traffic conditions, local points of interest such as closest or popular places to eat, you can find sports scores and biographies.

You can find Cortana by clicking in the search field on the task bar. Once you do that, her window will appear.

Using Cortana

Tap/Click the microphone icon, located on the right hand side of the search field on the task bar.

If you have it enabled, you can also get Cortana's attention by saying, "Hey Cortana!"

To enable this feature, tap in Cortana's search field 'ask me anything', tap the settings icon, and turn the slider to 'on' under 'hey cortana'.

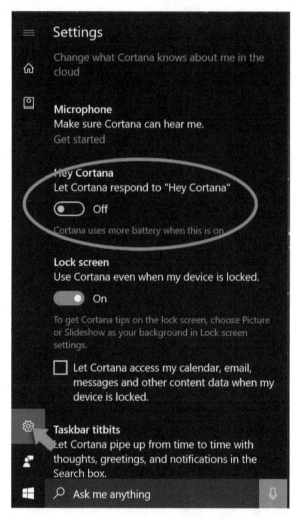

Now whenever you need Cortana, just say "Hey Cortana!" or tap the mic icon in the 'ask me anything' field and ask her a question.

Once you have gotten Cortana's attention, she will start listening to what you say. You'll see something like this. Notice the word 'listening' in the search field.

Try some of the following voice commands. You may need to change some of the names.

- *"Call Sister at home"*
- *"Send text to Sophie: When are you coming to play?"*
- *"Create a meeting with Claire at 2pm tomorrow"*
- *"Make Note: Pick up kids, take dog for walk, feed kids, buy milk and ice-cream on way home"*
- *"Show me restaurants nearby"*
- *"What's the forecast for this weekend?"*
- *"How do I get to Liverpool One?" or "Show me directions to Liverpool One."*

Other Features

Cortana also has some extra options located on the tool bar down the left hand side of the window.

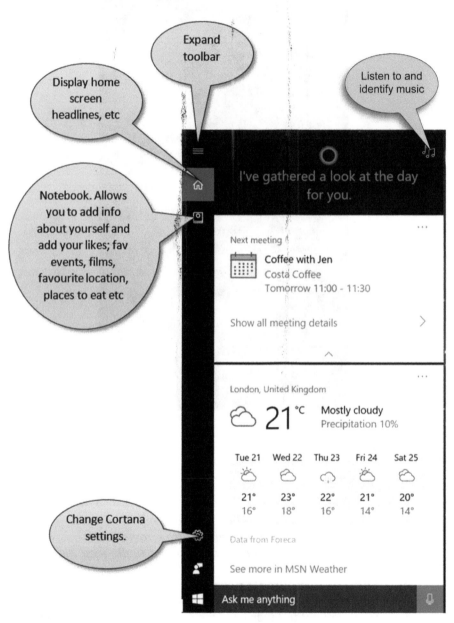

Notebook is Cortana's book of information about you. You can add and edit areas of interest from your daily routine, news and headlines, music, weather, food, lifestyle and so on. Tap the notebook icon on the tool bar and scroll through the categories: eat & drink, events, films & TV etc. Edit the details according to your personal tastes, for example, add Chinese or Italian favourite foods in the 'Eat & Drink' section.

You can add reminders using Cortana, just ask her to remind you of something, simply by tapping the mic icon on the taskbar and say it using your voice.

Try something like: "Hey Cortana, remind me to pick Claire up today at 4:30pm."

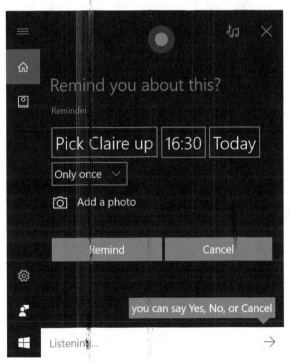

Cortana will confirm your reminder and ask you if it sounds good. You can respond by saying, 'yes' or 'no'. If you say 'yes', she will store your reminder in your reminders list. If you say 'no', she will ask you what you want to change; reminder, date or time. Change them by speaking the word, then speaking the amendment.

With Cortana music, she can identify music playing just by listening. She will then search for it. Can be a useful feature if you hear a song and what to know what it is or where you can get a copy.

Just tap the music icon on the tool bar and she begins listening...

If Cortana knows the song, she'll find it for you.

You can tap or click on this song to purchase a copy from the App Store.

Customise Cortana

You can customise Cortana in the settings pane.

To do this, click the settings icon on the tool bar circled above.

From here you can change your name and set different preferences. You can turn Cortana off or on, if you'd rather not use voice.

Scroll down the rest of the settings, and adjust them accordingly.

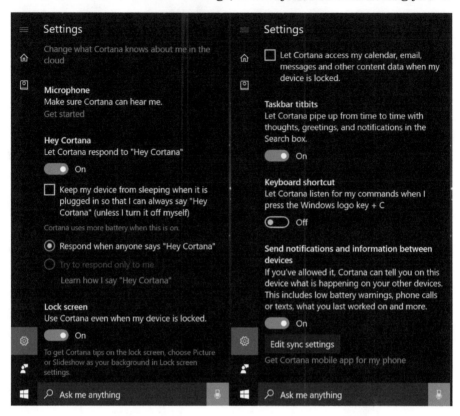

The functions are pretty well explained on the settings page, so have a read through.

A few things worth noting. If you're having a few issues with Cortana not hearing you, tap 'get started' under 'microphone' and run through the mic settings to make sure Cortana is receiving an audio signal.

For additional security and to prevent Cortana responding to anyone, you can train Cortana to respond to you only. Tap "learn how to 'say Hey Cortana!'" Then tap 'start' to run through the test phrases. You might need to tap the mic icon on the search bar if she isn't picking up your voice.

It's not advisable to allow Cortana to access calendar, email or messages when your device is locked - could be a security risk if someone else gets hold of your phone.

Sending notifications and info between devices is handy if you have a Windows phone, tablet and or a PC. If for example you receive a text or phone call and you're working on your PC and don't hear your phone ring, a notification will pop up on your PC informing you.

You might want to adjust the SafeSearch settings, this filters out pornography, suicide/self harm, drugs, criminal and malicious content. Either set to 'moderate' or 'strict'. This also helps to keep Cortana from returning potentially unsafe websites.

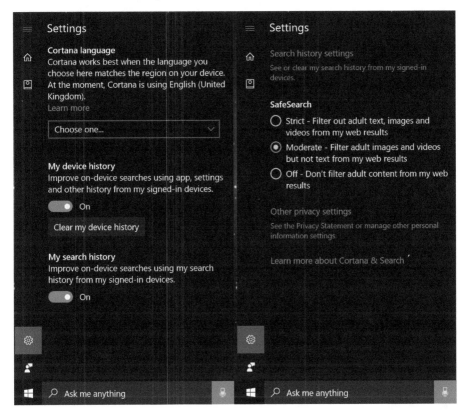

Most of them you probably won't have to change much.

Chapter 4

Windows 10 Tablets

Windows 10 is designed to run on a tablet computer and has a mode called 'tablet mode' that enables Windows to optimise the interface for touch screen users.

This means that the start menu takes up the whole screen, and apps run full screen to make them clearer and easier to use on a small touch sensitive screen rather than using a mouse.

You won't see the desktop in tablet mode but you can still use your desktop apps such as word, it will just run full screen instead of in a window.

Other than these differences, Windows 10 runs more or less the same as on a desktop or laptop.

Using a Tablet

You can easily switch to tablet mode, where apps show up full screen and are a bit larger to make it easier to navigate using touch.

You can see that in tablet mode everything opens up in full screen. The start menu becomes a start screen allowing you to tap directly on the tiles rather than using the mouse.

In desktop mode, you see the start menu and everything runs in a window which is easier with a point and click keyboard and mouse interface.

133

This is what you'll see if you are running Windows 10 on a tablet in tablet mode.

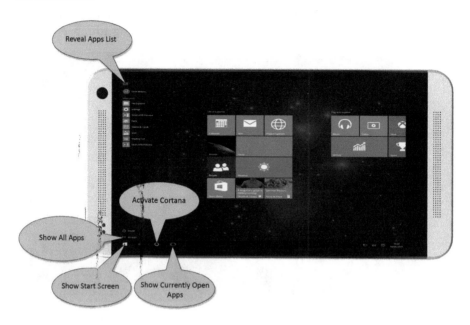

Along the left hand side you have a list of apps. Tap the hamburger icon on the very top left of the screen to reveal the list.

On the right hand side of the start screen you will see an array or coloured tiles. These represent your apps. You can tap these to start them up.

Along the bottom of the start screen, you'll see a black bar, this is the task bar. From here you can tap the start screen icon, start Cortana personal assistant, tap the task view icon to show currently open apps.

Customising your Start Screen

You can customise your start screen by resizing or moving tiles around. Just tap on the tile and slide your finger across the screen to where you want to place the tile.

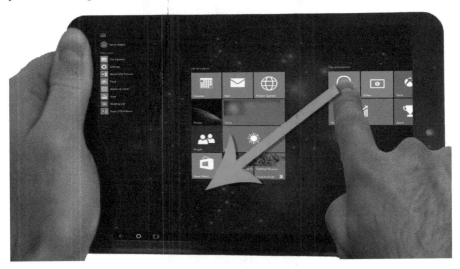

You can also drag your most used apps from the app list on the left hand side of the screen.

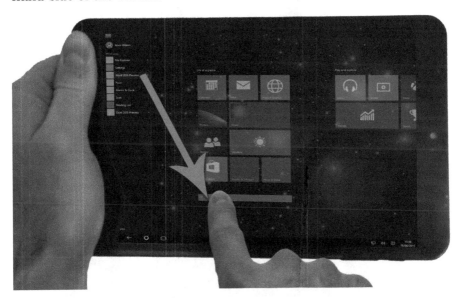

Tap 'all apps' on the bottom left if you don't see them all.

135

You can also resize tiles. To do this, tap on the tile with your finger, and hold until the little icons appear.

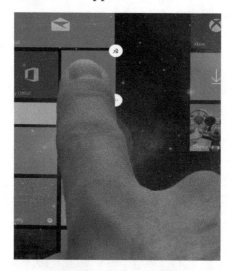

Tap the icon with the three little dots.

From the pop up menu tap resize.

From the slide out menu tap the size you want: small, medium, wide or large.

Gestures for Touch Screens

On your tablet's touch screen, you can use various gestures using your forefinger and thumb

One Finger Tap

Tapping with one finger is equivalent to clicking with your mouse, usually to select something. Tapping twice with your finger is the same as double clicking with the mouse and is usually used to start an app.

One Finger Tap and Hold

Tapping on the screen with your finger and holding it there for a second or two, is equivalent to using the right click with the mouse and usually invokes a context menu.

Three Finger Tap

Tapping on the screen with three fingers at the same time will invoke Cortana personal assistant. This doesn't work on all tablets.

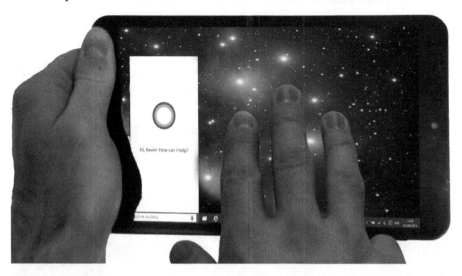

Four Finger Tap

Tapping on the screen with four fingers at a time will invoke your action centre with your options, messages and notifications. This doesn't work on all tablets.

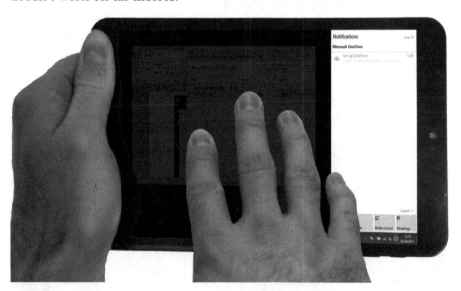

One Finger Slide

Tapping on an object and sliding your finger over the glass without lifting your finger, is the same as click and drag with the mouse. Use this to move objects such as windows and icons around the screen.

Two Finger Pinch

Pinch when used with your forefinger and thumb you can use to zoom into documents or maps and enlarge pages by zooming into and out of the screen.

Scroll

If you tap and move two fingers over the glass as shown below you can scroll up & down documents and pages.

Three Finger Swipe Up

Swiping three fingers upwards will show all the apps currently open on your device. This doesn't work on all Windows 10 tablets.

Three Finger Swipe Left/Right

Swiping three fingers left and right across the screen will flick through open applications running on your device.

Swipe from the Left Edge

Does the same as 'three finger swipe up'. Swipe from the left edge of the screen gives you your timeline/taskview; a thumbnail list of open apps. Tap on the thumbnail to switch to the app.

Swipe from the Right Edge

Swipe from the right edge of the screen opens your action centre.

Two Finger Rotate

Use your forefinger and thumb to rotate images or maps on the screen.

On-screen Keyboard

Your on-screen keyboard will appear whenever you tap inside a text field.

To bring up the keyboard at any other time, tap the icon on the right hand side of the task bar. Note this icon wont appear if you have a keyboard plugged into your tablet.

You can also change the layout of your keyboard. Do this by tapping the keyboard icon located on the bottom right of your on screen keyboard.

From here, you can split your keyboard, so half appears on the left and the other half appears on the right; can be more comfortable to type.

The on-screen keyboard also has a hand writing recognition feature that instead of typing, you can actually write words and sentences using your pen or finger.

You can do this by tapping on the icon located on the bottom right of your on-screen keyboard, and selecting the pen and pad icon.

For example, when saving my screen sketch image, I can write the file name instead of typing it, and the text appears in the text field.

You can even use this feature in Word processing apps; write instead of typing.

Keyboards & Cases

If you own a tablet similar to the one pictured here, you can buy cases that include a keyboard.

This allows you to use the device as a tablet but can also double as a touch screen notebook. When you plug your keyboard in, Windows 10 goes into desktop mode.

When you detach your keyboard, you will get a message like the one shown here. Tap the message to enter tablet mode.

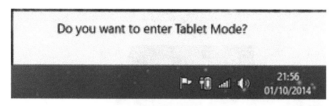

Surface tablets have keyboards that magnetically slot into place as shown below.

Keyboards usually connect to your tablet using bluetooth and sometimes with a micro usb cable.

Surface tablets have their own keyboards that slot in magnetically and connect via the keyboard connector or via bluetooth.

If your keyboard is bluetooth, you will have to 'pair' it with your tablet.

Go to settings -> devices -> bluetooth.

You'll see a list of discovered devices. Select your keyboard name from the list, then click 'pair'. Make sure your keyboard is powered on.

The device should connect to your tablet, you may be asked to enter a code, as in the example below. Enter the code on the keyboard, if this is the case, then hit enter.

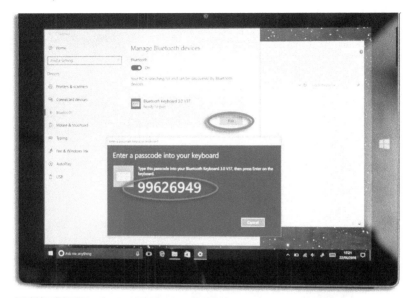

The procedure may vary from keyboard to keyboard, so check the instructions that came from the manufacturer.

Pens

You can buy pens and styluses to use with your tablet. These come in useful for Windows Ink & OneNote, as well as any art apps out there that you can find in the App Store.

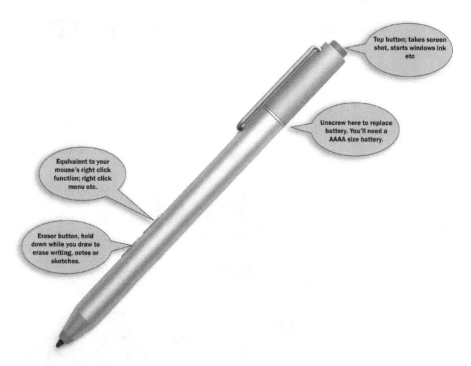

Top button; takes screen shot, starts windows ink etc

Unscrew here to replace battery. You'll need a AAAA size battery.

Equivalent to your mouse's right click function; right click menu etc.

Erasor button, hold down while you draw to erase writing, notes or sketches.

These come in various types but the ones that work best have bluetooth capability, meaning you can pair the pen with your tablet giving you extra features such as shortcut buttons, mouse button equivalents and so on.

First put your pen into 'pairing mode'. To do this, hold down the top button for about 10 seconds, until the little green light on the side of the pen starts flashing.

On your tablet, go to settings -> devices -> bluetooth and select your pen from the list. Turn bluetooth on if you need to.

Click 'pair'.

Your pen will automatically pair itself with your tablet.

Other Accessories

You can buy little USB adapters that plug into the side of your tablet. This allows you to plug in standard USB devices such as a mouse, digital camera, card reader, printer, etc.

Chapter 5

Internet, Email & Communication

Windows 10 has a new web browser called Edge and is installed by default. It has new features that allow you to annotate websites, share and make notes.

We'll also take a brief look at two other browsers, Google Chrome and FireFox. These are a good alternative to Microsoft Edge.

Windows 10 also has revamped mail and calendar apps, where you can add all your email accounts, whether it's Google, Yahoo, Microsoft account or any other account, you can have them all in one place.

We'll take a look at these later in this chapter. Also we'll take a look at how to get started using Skype for making calls.

Lets begin by taking a look at Microsoft's new browser, Edge.

Microsoft Edge Web Browser

Originally codenamed "Spartan", Microsoft Edge is built for the modern web, is a more lightweight web browser, replaces Internet Explorer in Windows 10 and has had a few tweaks in the Spring Creator's Update.

Edge integrates with Cortana assistant and OneDrive, also has annotation tools, reading modes and sharing tools.

Microsoft has also introduced a new icon for the Edge Browser in Windows 10. You can find the icon either on your task bar or on your start menu.

Lets take a look at what Edge looks like. Edge has a much cleaner interface than Internet Explorer.

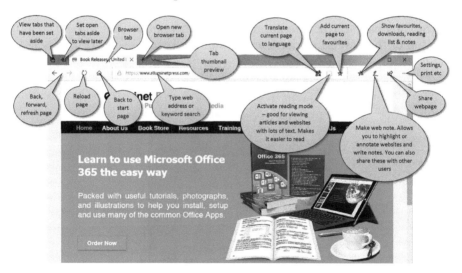

Along the top of the window you will find your address bar where you can enter search keywords or website addresses.

You can add websites to favourites, show favourites, make annotations on web pages, both handwritten or typed.

You can access all these features by tapping or clicking on the icons on your tool bar at the top of the screen.

Bookmarks

To bookmark a page, click the star icon at the top of the screen.

In the dialog box that appears type in a name for the website

Where it says 'save in'. Click the arrow on the right hand side to expand the options. Select 'favourites' to save the website to your favourites list - this appears when you click the 'show favourites' icon. Click 'favourites bar' to the website to the favourites bar that appears along the top of the screen under the website address.

You can also create folders to organise your favourites. Click on 'create new folder' and enter a name in the 'folder name' field.

To revisit your bookmarked sites, click your favourites icon.

This will open your favourites list. You'll see the website you bookmarked appear on the list.

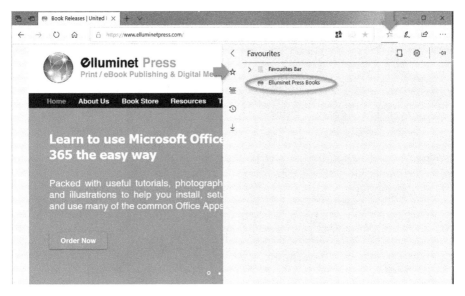

You can drag the websites up and down in the list, to reorder them; or you can drag them into the yellow folders. To create a new yellow folder, right click on the favourites sidebar and from the popup menu select 'create new folder' then type in name.

The 'favourites bar' appears along the top of your Edge browser underneath the navigation buttons and the address bar. This is the place to put all the websites you visit most often.

By default, this bar is hidden, but you can turn it on quite easily. Tap the three dots on the top right, then tap settings. From the settings menu, go down to 'show the favourites bar'. Switch this to 'on'.

Annotations & Notes

You can enter annotation mode by clicking on the icon on the tool bar

You will notice a new tool bar appears along the top of your screen.

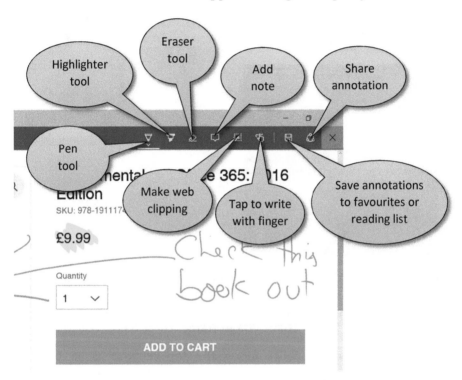

Starting from the left hand side of the tool bar, you have a pen tool.

The next icon across is a highlighter pen.

An eraser tool that allows you to rub out annotations you have drawn.

A note tool that allows you to type annotations in if you can't had write them.

A web clipping tool that allows you to copy a section of the webpage including your annotations to the clipboard where you can paste into a word processing or note taking application.

Pen Tool

Select the pen tool with your mouse or finger/stylus (if using touch interface), then select a colour and pen thickness (size).

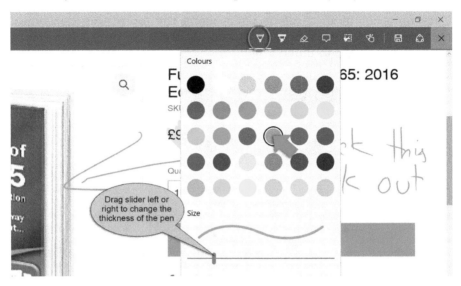

Draw directly on the web page as illustrated below.

You can highlight headings, draw arrows or handwrite text when doing research for example. Or perhaps you want to highlight a part of a webpage you found useful so it's easier to find when you come back to it. You can save these annotations to your favourites or send them to friends.

Highlighter Pen

Use the highlighter tool to highlight different words or paragraphs on the web page.

Click on a colour in a colour pallet along the top of the drop-down, then use the slider underneath to adjust the size; drag left to make smaller, drag right to make larger.

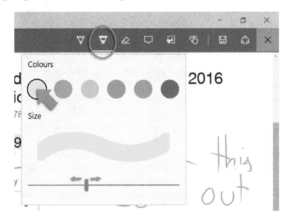

You can draw directly on the screen with your finger or stylus to highlight any text as shown below

There is also an eraser tool so you can rub out any annotations you have made.

Typed Notes

You can also add typed notes with the next icon across. Tap on the note icon, then tap on the webpage, where you want the note to point to.

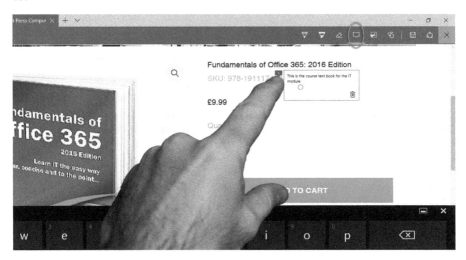

Then type your notes in the text box that appears, either using the on screen keyboard or an attached keyboard. I find attached keyboards easier to type on

Saving Notes

You can save or share all these annotations using the two icons on the right hand side of the tool bar.

Use the first icon to save the annotations into your favourites or reading list. You can also use the second icon to share your annotated web page via email, print it out etc.

Reading Mode

Some websites, especially those with a lot of text can be difficult to print or read on screen.

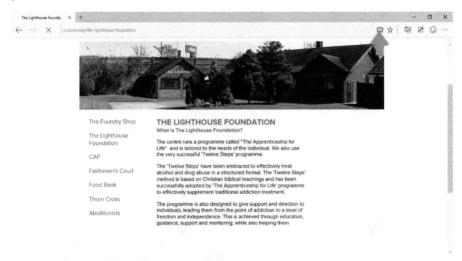

Edge has a reading mode that can be quite useful when reading articles on websites.

Also some websites do not print particularly well since they are designed to be viewed on screen. So by using the reading mode you can print your website article in a more printer friendly fashion.

Page Translator

You can translate any page into another language. To do this, click the translate icon on the top of your browser window.

In the drop down box, Edge will auto detect the current language and display it in the 'from' field. In the 'to' field, select the language you want to translate the page into.

Lets try Spanish...

Here you can see Edge has attempted a translation. Translations aren't 100% accurate but will give you the general idea.

This is a useful tool if you come across a website that isn't in your own language, you can quickly translate it using this feature.

More Options

There are some hidden menu options in Edge that you can access by clicking on the 3 dots on the far right hand side of the screen. This will reveal a drop down menu

From the menu, you can print the current page, make the text bigger using the zoom function.

You can share the current web page via email or social media by clicking 'share'.

You can search for a particular word on the current web page by clicking 'find on page'.

You can print the current page.

You can adjust settings such as security and privacy.

Print a Page

You can print the current web page by clicking 'print' from the 'more options' icon indicated below.

If you click print from the menu, you will see another dialog box appear asking you what printer you want to print to and number of copies etc.

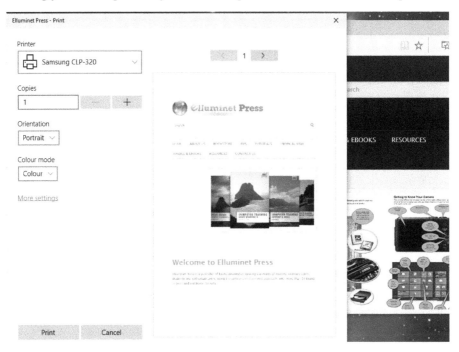

Select the printer from the printer box, enter number of copies if needed.

You can also print portrait or landscape

Select colour mode or black and white

Click print when you are happy with the preview of the printed page shown on the right hand side.

Pin a Website to the Start Menu

A useful feature of Microsoft Edge is the ability to pin a website shortcut onto your start menu.

To do this, you need to open the website in Microsoft Edge. In this example, I am going to add Google Maps, as it's a website I use quite often for travel and finding directions.

Click the icon with the three dots, on the top right of your window.

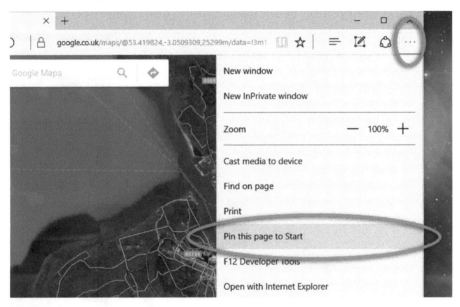

From the drop down menu, select 'pin this page to start'. Click 'yes' to the question 'do you want to pin this tile to start'.

You will find your web page appear as a tile on the start menu. It usually has the Microsoft Edge logo with the name of the website underneath, as shown below.

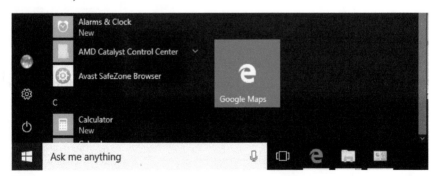

Pin Website to TaskBar

A useful feature of Microsoft Edge is the ability to pin a website shortcut onto your taskbar. You should only really use this feature for websites you visit very often, as you can quite easily fill up your taskbar with clutter. Perhaps if you use a web based email or facebook - create a taskbar short cut.

To do this, open the website you want to pin in Microsoft Edge.

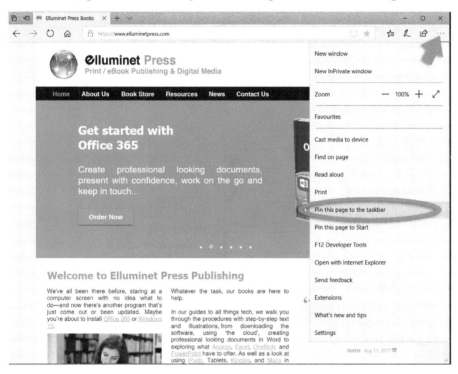

You'll see the website link appear on your task bar. The icon depends on the website's own icon.

Change your Start Page

It's useful to change the start page to automatically go to a page you use most often. Google search is a popular option.

To change the start page, click the 'more options' icon on the top right of your screen. From the menu, select 'settings'.

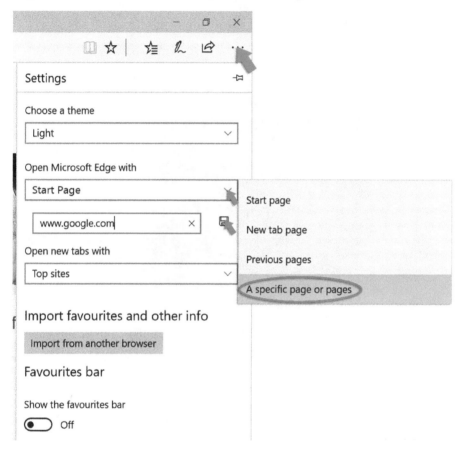

Go down and click on the drop down box that says 'start page'. From the menu select 'a specific page or pages'.

In the 'enter a url' field, type in the web address of the website. In this example I am going to add Google search.

www.google.com

Tab Preview Bar

The tab preview bar gives you a thumbnail preview of the webpage currently open on that tab.

To preview your open website tabs, click the tab preview icon to the right of the tab list, as shown below.

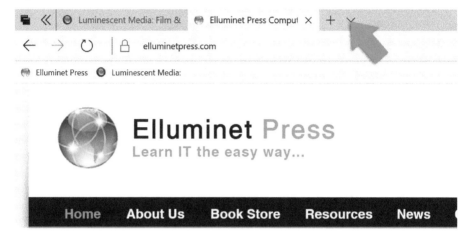

The tab bar will expand to show you a preview of your currently open website tabs.

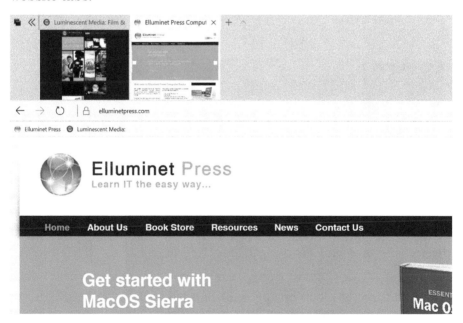

Click on these tabs to switch to that website.

Set Aside Tabs

Microsoft Edge browser opens websites up in tabs. This feature allows you set aside website tabs you have open, so you can restore and look at them later. This helps to avoid visual clutter if you happen to open lots of tabs at the same time.

To set aside open website tabs, click the 'set aside' icon on the top left of your screen.

You'll see all your open website tabs disappear and a new blank website tab open up. This is almost like putting sites 'on the shelf' to look at later.

To view the website tabs you have set aside, click the icon on the top left of your screen to open the sidebar.

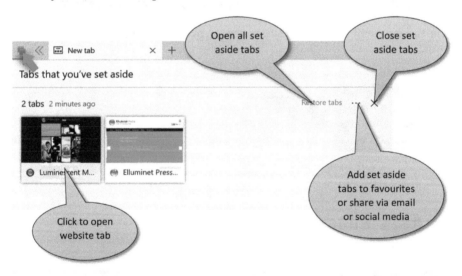

In the sidebar that opens you'll see a list of thumbnail previews of the website tabs you have set aside. Click on these to go back to the website.

Click the three dot icon on the right hand side. From the drop down, you can share the tabs via email or social media, or you can add them to your favourites.

166

Edge Extensions

Extensions add functionality to the Edge Browser.

To add extensions to Edge, click the 'more' icon on the top right of your screen and select 'extensions'.

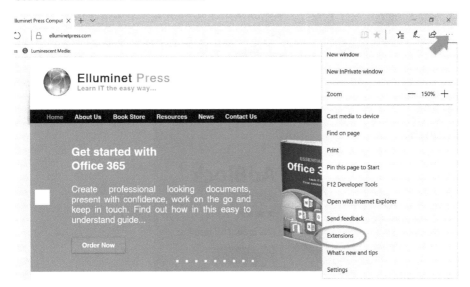

From the sidebar that opens up, you'll see all your installed extensions. To get new extensions click 'get extensions from the store'. At the time of writing there are only a few extensions available, but the library is expected to grow over time.

In this example, I'm going to add the Adblock extension. So click 'AdBlock'.

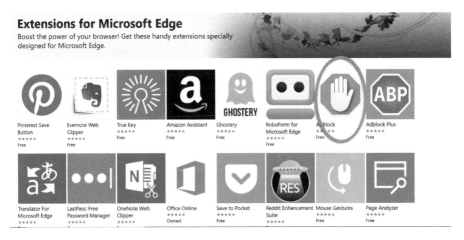

From the extension details page, click 'get'.

The extension will start to download. Once it has installed, click 'launch'.

You'll see a prompt telling you there is a new extension, click 'turn on' to enable it.

You can access your extensions anytime, just click the 'more' icon on the top right of your screen and select 'extensions' from the menu. Click on the extension name to change its settings.

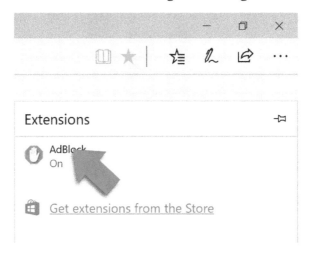

Here, you can enable/disable the extension and if you click 'options', you'll see a webpage with some preferences you can adjust.

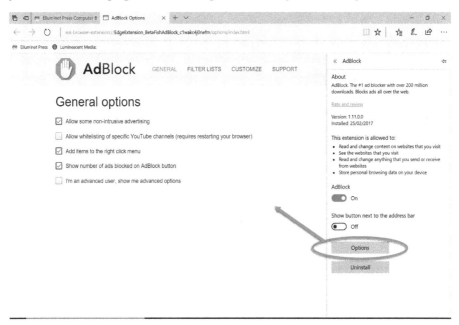

To completely remove the extension just click 'uninstall'.

Web Payments & Microsoft Wallet

Microsoft Wallet is Microsoft's answer to Apple Pay and will be available on Windows 10 Phones. Just look for the icon on your start screen.

You can pay for things with your Microsoft Wallet anywhere you see the contactless symbol or Microsoft Wallet logo.

If this is the first time you're running Wallet, tap 'Sounds good! Sign in' then enter your Microsoft Account email address and password.

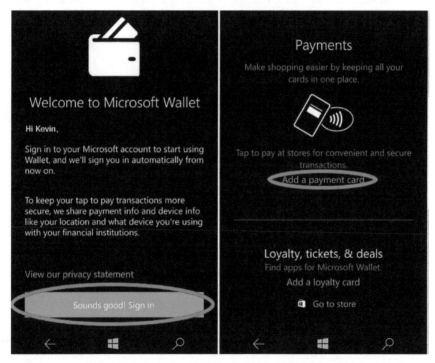

You can add your cards to your Microsoft Wallet by scanning them with your phone's on-board camera. To do this, on the next screen tap 'add a payment card'

Tap 'scan your card'.

Now, position your card in the frame as shown below.

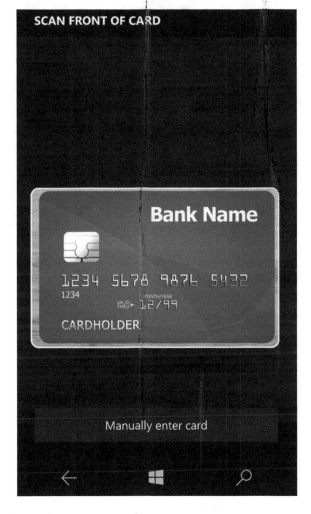

Tap screen to capture your card.

Once the card has been captured, run through the process to verify your card. You'll need to enter the security code from the back of your card when prompted.

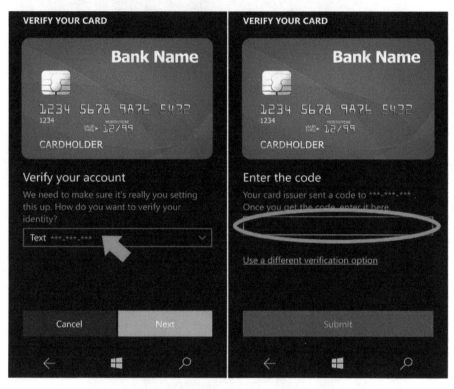

Select a verification method. This is usually via text message to a phone registered to your Microsoft Account. You can also use to send it to your Microsoft Account email address. Tap 'Next'.

Enter the code sent to your phone and tap 'submit'.

Tap 'go to my cards'.

Now when you're in any participating store, launch your wallet, select a card and hold your phone next to the card reader.

Other Browsers Worth Noting

There are a few other browsers that are worth taking note of. These are Google Chrome and FireFox. I prefer Chrome personally but why not give them both a try. Either of these two browsers make great alternatives to Microsoft Edge.

Google Chrome

Google Chrome is a fast and streamlined browser and gives access to its App Store so you can run Google Apps on your browser, connect to Google Drive, edit and save documents using Google's word processor, spreadsheet and presentation apps as well as browsing the web using Google itself.

You can download Google Chrome from

`www.google.com/chrome/browser`

Hit the download button. Click 'accept and install'. Go to your downloads folder and double click 'chromesetup.exe'

Follow the on screen instructions to install the browser.

Once Chrome has loaded, click the profile icon on the top right and enter your Google account username and password.

This is the same account that you use for Gmail if you have one.

You can use Chrome without a Google account, but you won't get any of the personalised features or be able to add apps to Chrome from the Chrome Store.

Chapter 5: Internet, Email & Communication

You can use Google Chrome in a similar way to Edge. This is Chrome's Start screen. You can type in your Google Search or type a URL if you know it into the search bar. Along the bottom you'll also see your most visited websites.

Let's take a closer look at Chrome's interface.

FireFox

FireFox is a free browser developed by the Mozilla Corporation and is fast and secure.

You can download FireFox from

`www.firefox.com`

Hit the 'free download' button.

Click 'run', if prompted by your browser.

If you don't get a prompt, go to your downloads folder and double click 'Firefox Setup Stub.exe'

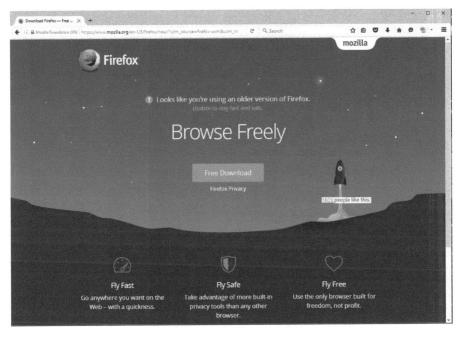

Follow the on screen instructions to install the browser.

Mail App

You can start the Mail App by tapping or clicking on the mail icon on your start menu.

If this is the first time you are using this app, you may be asked to add your email account.

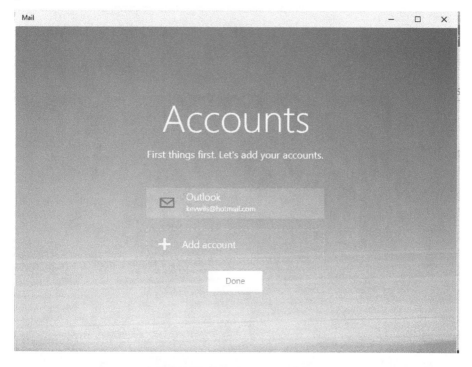

If you are using your Microsoft Account, mail app usually finds it as shown above.

Select this email account and click done.

Adding Other Email Accounts

If you have another email account such as Gmail or Yahoo you can add these too.

To do this click the settings icon on the bottom left of the screen.

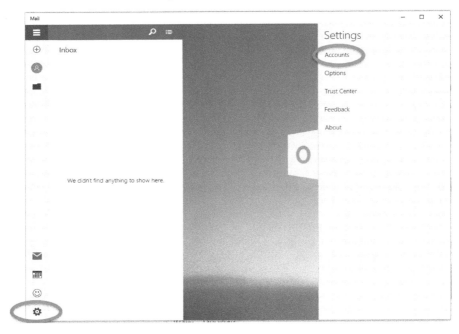

Click 'manage accounts', then 'add account' and enter the email username and password given to you by the account provider (Google, Yahoo, Apple, etc).

If your provider isn't in the list above click 'other account'.

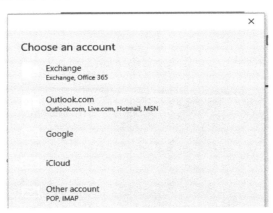

In this example, I want to add a Gmail account. So click on Google and in the dialog box that appears, enter your Gmail address and password.

Scroll down and click 'accept' at the bottom of the confirmation dialogue box.

All your email accounts will appear under the accounts section on the left hand side of the screen.

Reading Mail

When you open mail app it will check for email, any new messages will appear in your inbox.

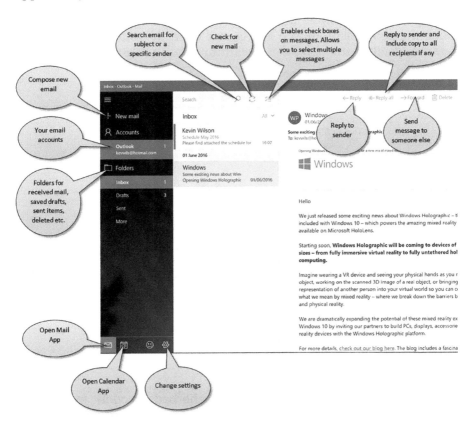

Click on the message in your inbox. The contents will be displayed in the reading pane on the right hand side.

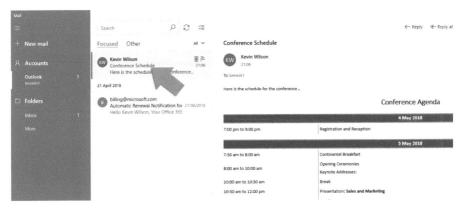

Writing a New Message

To start a new message, click 'new mail' on the top left hand side of the main screen.

First you need to enter the person's email address in the 'To' field. Click the people icon on the far right to open up your contacts. Scroll down and select the person you want to send the email to.

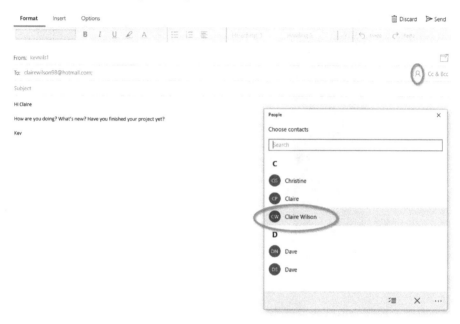

Add a subject, then type your email in the body section. In the body section, you can use the normal text formatting tools such as bold, change the font colour or size and so on, using the format tool bar as you can see below.

Hit 'send' on the top right to send your email message.

180

Reply to a Message

To reply to the message, click the reply icon at the top of the screen.

You'll see a screen that looks a bit like a word processor. Here you can type in your message. Your message will appear at the top. The original message will be appended to the end of the email.

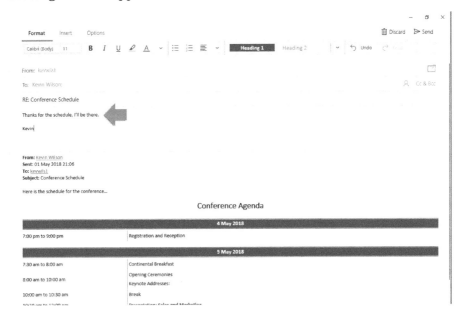

You can use the basic formatting tools. You can make text bold - select the text and click the 'B' icon on the toolbar. Or you can make text into bullet points. Select the text and click the bullet icon.

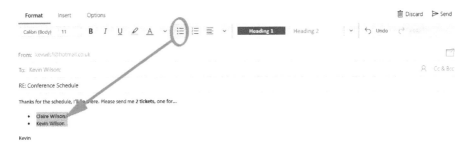

Adding Attachments

To attach a file, click 'insert' then select 'files'. Select the file you want to attach. Use this option to attach files such as documents, videos, music or photos.

Select your file from the dialog box. Hold down the control key to select multiple files. Click 'open' when you're done.

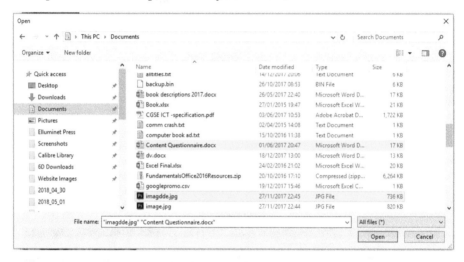

These attachments will be added to the end of the email.

Once you are done, click 'send' on the top right.

Inserting Images

Inserting images is a little different from adding an attachment. When you insert an image, you insert it into the body of the email message so it appears inline with the text.

In your email message, click 'insert'. From the options, select 'pictures'.

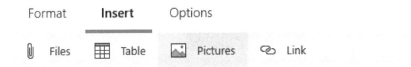

Select your picture from the dialog box. Hold down the control key if you're selecting more than one picture. Click 'insert'.

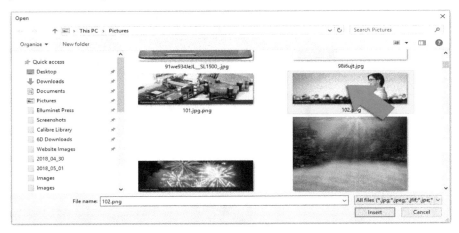

Click the 'send' icon on the top right when you're done.

Calendar App

The calendar app links in with the mail app, you can find it on your start menu. It will either have a calendar icon or it will be displaying the current date.

If this is the first time you are using this app, you may be asked to add your email account.

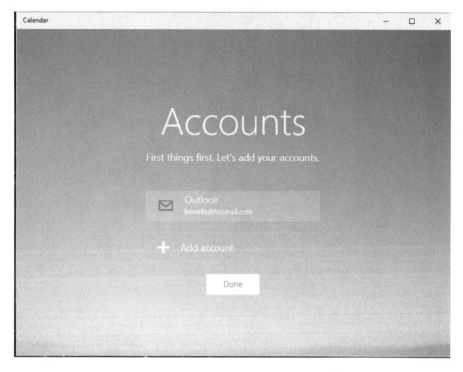

If you are using a Microsoft account, calendar app usually finds it for you. If this is the case select the account and click done.

If you use another email account click add account and enter your username/email and password details given to you by the account provider.

Once you have done that, you will see your main screen.

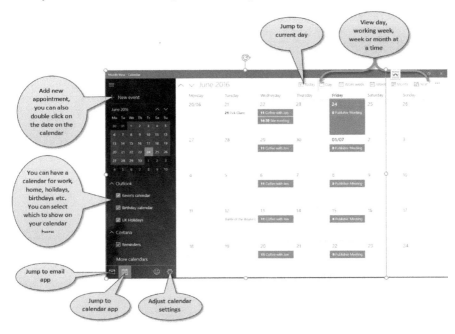

You can add events and appointments by clicking on the 'new event' button or double clicking on the date in the calendar.

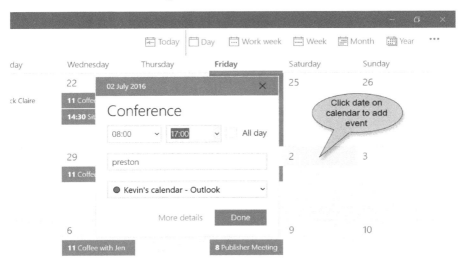

Type the location where you are meeting. Un-tick 'all day' and enter start and estimated finishing times. Unless it's an all day event.

Hit 'more details'.

You can add notes and any details about the event in the large text box at the bottom of the screen.

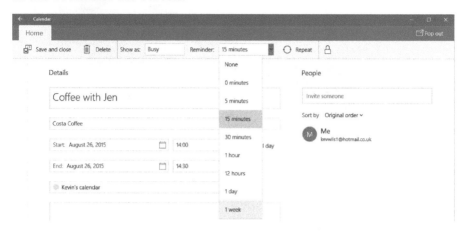

You can add a reminder too, by changing the reminder field. You can set it from none, 5 mins before, 15 mins before, a day before and so on. Reminders will pop up in your action centre as they occur.

Home

Save and close   Delete   Show as: Busy   Reminder: 1 day

Details

Conference

Preston

Start: 02 July 2016   08:00

End: 02 July 2016   17:00

| None |
| 0 minutes |
| 5 minutes |
| 15 minutes |
| 30 minutes |
| 1 hour |
| 12 hours |
| 1 day |
| 1 week |

If the event is recurring, eg happens once a week or once a month, you can set this by clicking 'repeat'.

Under the 'repeat' section, you can set the event to occur on a daily, weekly, monthly and yearly basis. This saves you having to enter it for every occurrence.

Next, change any specifics such as what day a week/month the event occurs. In this example, the event occurs every week on a Tuesday.

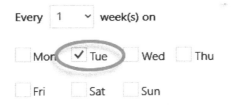

If the event ran every two weeks on Tuesday, we would change the top line to every 2 weeks.

In the next bit, you can set the date your recurring event ends. Eg if it is a course it might be weekly for 6 months or a year.

Hit 'save and close' on the top left of the screen when you're done.

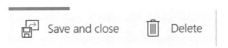

People App

The People App brings communication to the forefront of Windows 10. You can pin the people you communicate with the most, directly to your task bar. You can find the People App on your start menu

When the People App opens up, you'll see a list of your contacts.

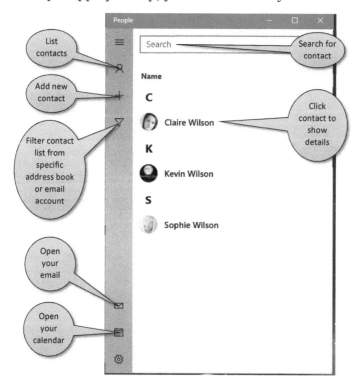

Edit Contact

You can click on any of the contacts in your list to view or edit their contact information.

Here I've clicked on Claire's contact. In her window you'll see her contact details, plus upcoming calendar events she's been invited to or involved in and recent messages. Click 'see more' to see all of these.

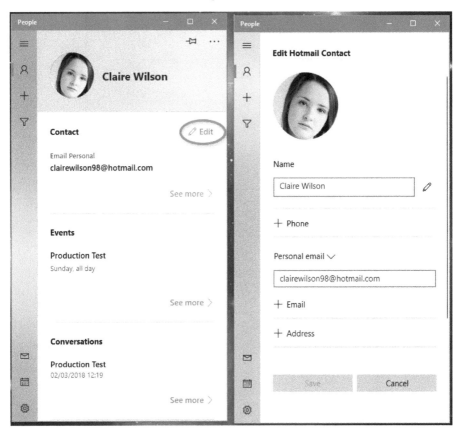

To edit her contact details, click 'edit'. In the new window you can edit her name, add phone, email addresses and physical address.

Click the plus sign next to the one you want to add.

Click 'save' when you're done.

Pin Contacts

To pin a contact to your task bar, right click on the contact's name and select 'pin to taskbar' from the popup menu. Select 'pin' from the conformation box that appears.

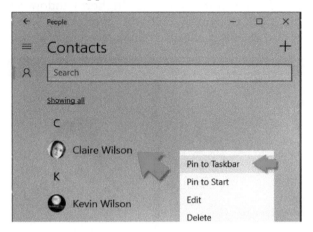

You'll see the person's profile picture appear on the bottom right of your taskbar. Click on the profile picture to open up their window.

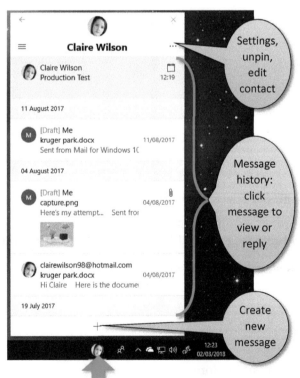

Share Files with Contacts

You can drag files to the person's icon on the task bar if you want to share with them. If I wanted to share this file with Claire, I can drag and drop the file from file explorer onto her icon on the taskbar.

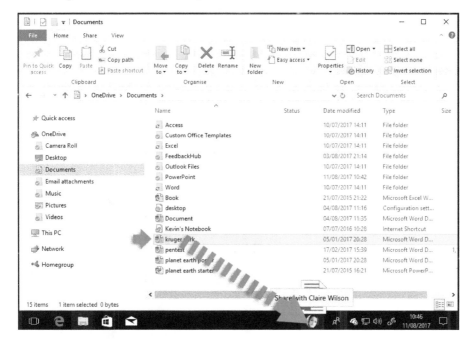

The People App will open a contact window using your default method of contact - in this example, email.

Add a message if you wish, then click 'send' to send the message.

Skype

Microsoft has now integrated Skype into Windows 10. You can use it along with your Microsoft Account and your mobile/cell phone number.

You can access it by double clicking on the icon on your start menu. If you can't find it, type 'skype' into the search bar on the task bar.

Making a Call

You can either select someone's name from your call history, or select Phonebook or the People App, click on the contact's name and on their profile click 'Video Call' to place a Skype call.

The video call option will only appear on their profile if they are able to receive video calls.

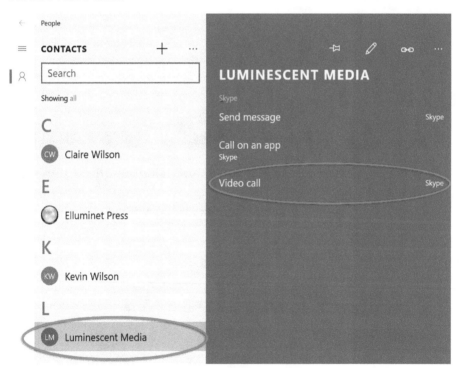

Once you click on Video Call, skype will open and attempt to connect to that person's skype account.

When the call comes through, the other person will get an alert on the bottom right of their screen. They can either accept or decline the call.

In the demo below, the tablet is calling the user logged on to the laptop, you can see the call screen on the tablet and the incoming call alert on the laptop.

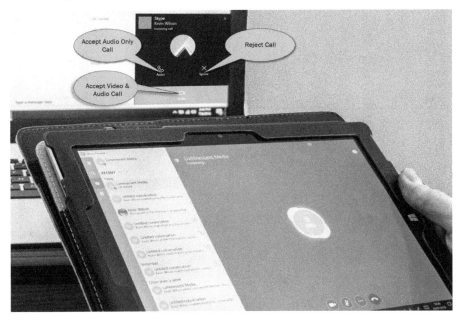

Once the other user picks up the call, you'll see an image of them on your screen.

You will also see a thumbnail view of yourself on the bottom right of the screen.

Along the bottom of the 'in call' screen you have 4 icons.

From left to right you have:

- Enable/disable web cam,
- Mute/un-mute microphone,
- Extra options (share your screen with another user, add another person to current call & speaker phone)
- End call.

In the demo below, Claire logged onto the tablet and placed a skype call to the user logged onto the laptop.

You can see on the laptop screen, the person you're talking to will appear in the large section of the window.

You will see a thumbnail view of yourself in the bottom right hand corner.

Screen Sharing

Another cool feature of Skype is the ability to share your desktop with the user you are having a skype call with.

This is a great way to keep in touch with people you don't see very often, as well as friends and family. It makes a great collaboration tool for business users too and enables you to share your screen to show photos, word documents, presentations etc.

In the demo below, the tablet on the right, is sharing its screen with the user logged onto the laptop. The tablet user is then able to launch any app, in this example, photos. Then the tablet user can open photos to show the other user.

The user on the laptop can see everything the tablet user is displaying on their screen.

Both users can still talk and see one another as if they were still in conversation. You'll see a thumbnail view of them in the bottom right hand corner of your screen.

To share your screen, make your video call as normal, then from the in call screen, tap the icon with the three dots.

From the menu that appears, click 'share screen'.

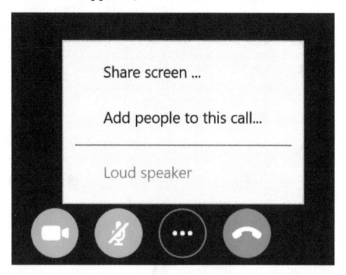

The other user will now be able to see everything on your screen.

Mobile Hotspot

Also known as tethering, this feature allows you to share your internet connection with your other devices and does this by creating a temporary WiFi hotspot. This can be useful if you have a 4G data connection on your phone but no WiFi available and need to access the internet on a tablet or laptop.

To enable your Wi-Fi hotspot, on your Windows Phone go to...

Settings App -> Network & Internet -> Mobile Hotspot

Flick the slider over to 'on'. Make a note of the network name and network password underneath.

On your laptop or tablet, tap on the WiFi icon on the right hand side of your taskbar. Windows 10 will scan for available WiFi networks. The network name you noted on your phone should appear. Tap on this network then tap 'connect'. Enter the password you noted on your phone and click 'next'.

197

Chapter 6

Multimedia

Windows 10 has a number of multimedia applications available.

There is an app to organise and enhance your digital photos whether it be from your phone or digital camera.

There is an app to take photographs using your phone/tablet.

There is an app to organise your music collection and a store for you to buy new music.

You can download and watch movies and television programmes which are available from the store.

Windows 10 doesn't come with the ability to play DVDs but you can download some software that will allow you to still enjoy your DVD collection.

Photos App

The photos app is a nice little way to organise your photos and works whether you are on a tablet, phone or desktop PC.

You can find the photos app on the start menu.

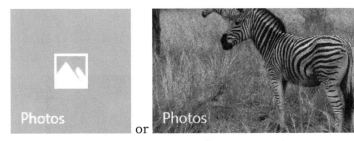

Photos app will import photos directly from your digital camera or on-board camera if you are using a tablet or phone.

You can also perform minor corrections and enhancements such as removing red-eye, lightening up a dark photograph or apply some simple effects such as sepia or black and white.

To do this, tap or click on an image, this will open the image in view mode.

Chapter 6: Multimedia

This will give you some options to share a photograph via email or social media, see the image full screen, edit it or delete it. You can tap the magic wand icon to perform some automatic adjustments such as brightness, contrast etc.

You can also tap the pencil icon to do your own editing and photo enhancements.

If you tap or click the pencil icon you will enter edit mode. In edit mode, you will see a panel open up on the right hand side. At the top of the panel you can tap 'crop and rotate' to crop your photo or rotate it. Underneath you have two categories of options. The first is enhance, and allows you to apply filters and effects to your photos. The second is adjust, and allows you to adjust the brightness, contrast, shadows, highlights and colour correction to your photos.

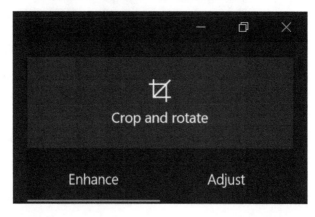

If I wanted to crop my zebra photo, I could do so using the crop icon at the top of the side panel. You'll notice a box appear around the photo. Click and drag the white circles to resize the box so it surrounds the part of the photo you want to keep, as shown below.

Tap 'done' when you're happy. You can also rotate your image to get it level. Drag the control handle, circled below, to line up the horizon with the lines on the grid, or any vertical or horizontal lines to level up the photo.

Tap 'done', when you're happy.

Also if you wanted to adjust the brightness, select the 'adjust' tab on the right hand panel, tap 'light', and all your lighting adjust tools will appear underneath (contrast, exposure, shadows and highlights), as shown in the illustration below.

Use the sliders underneath to adjust the levels.

Hit 'save' when you're done to save the adjustments you have made. The procedure is the same for all other adjustments, effects and fixes.

You can also post or share your favourites to facebook or email, just tap 'share'. In the example below, I posted this one on facebook.

Tap the back arrow on the top left of the screen to get back to your collections.

You can also draw on your photographs too using the 'draw icon' on the edit screen.

Draw with your pen or finger to annotate your photograph.

Along the top of your screen you'll see a tool bar. You can select from three different writing tools: a pen, a pencil, and a calligraphy pen.

The next icon along is an eraser. This allows you to use your pen or finger to rub out parts of your drawing.

The next icon along toggles between writing with your finger and writing with your pen stylus.

You can also save and share the photos with your annotations using the share and save icons.

Story Remix

A new feature called 'story remix', originally a stand alone app but now integrated into the Photos App, allows you to quickly and easily blend mixed reality, 3D, photos and videos into a video clip that you can share on social media, or use to promote an idea or business.

Creating Videos Automatically

To create a video, click 'collection' then click 'create'. From the drop down menu, select 'create custom video with music'.

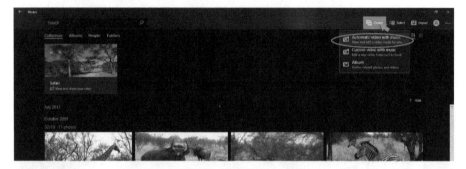

Click the photos/videos you want to include in your video.

Click 'create'.

Give your video a name

When it's finished, you'll be able to see a preview of the video remix has created..

If you don't like the style, you can click the 'remix it for me' button and Photos App will generate a new video.

To make any custom changes just click 'edit video' on the bottom right. This will take you to the custom edit screen where you can make changes to your video. See page 205.

If you're happy with the results, click 'export or share'. See page 214.

Creating Custom Videos

To create a video, click 'collection' then click 'create'. From the drop down menu, select 'create custom video with music'.

Click the photos/videos you want to include in your video.

Click 'create', when you're done.

You'll see the main editing screen. Lets take a look at the different parts.

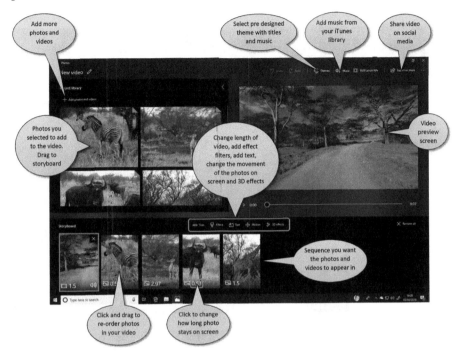

Top left, you'll see all the photos and videos you selected in the previous step.

On the top right you'll see some icons to add themes, music, as well as an export feature so you can share your creations.

Underneath that on the right hand side you'll see a large preview screen. This is a preview of your video. You can scrub through it using the progress bar underneath.

Along the bottom is your storyboard or timeline. This is the sequence of photos and videos that will make up your video.

Along the top of the storyboard are some icons that allow you to trim your sequence, add some photo filters, add text, motion effects and some 3D effects. These help to make your video more interesting for viewers to watch.

On the top left, you'll see all the photographs and videos you added at the beginning. You can drag and drop these onto the storyboard along the bottom of the screen.

Along the bottom, you'll see the order of photos/videos you have added. To reorder these, drag them across to the position in the sequence you want them.

Click the numbers on the bottom of each thumbnail on the storyboard to change the duration of each photo/video

Add Text Titles

You can add text to your video. First, select the photo you want the text to appear. In this example, I am going to add a title, so I'm going to select the first photo. Select a template from the bottom right (I'm going to choose 'electric'), type your title into the text field on the top right.

Select where you want the text to appear: centre, top, left; using the 'choose layout' section on the bottom right. Click 'done' on the top right when you're finished.

Add Music

Now, how about some music. Since this is a remix of our Safari trip, I'm going to use the 'road trip' music - seems appropriate. So select the music option on the top right of the screen, from the popup window select 'explorer'.

You can also add your own music if you prefer. Click on 'your music' then 'select a music file'.

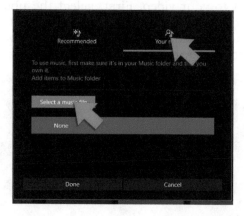

Navigate to your music folder on your computer - this is usually called 'music' and select a track.

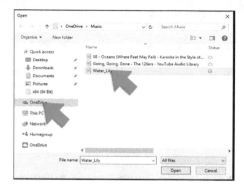

Select the track in the preview screen. Click 'done' when your happy.

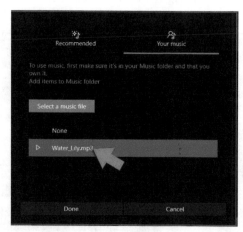

Slideshow Motion

To change the motion of your photographs in your slideshow, select the photo slide you want to change.

Now select a motion style from the options on the right hand side of the screen

Here you can select 'zoom in right', which will slow zoom into the right hand side of the image; or 'zoom in left' zooms into the left hand side of the image. These are useful if the subject in the photograph is on the left or right hand side of the image - helps draw attention to your subject. You can also pan across the image or zoom into the centre.

211

3D Effects

3D effects can only be added to video clips not still photographs. If you select a still photograph, the 3D effects button will be greyed out.

Click '3D Effects'.

Scrub to the part of the footage you want the effect to appear, using the progress bar underneath your video preview.

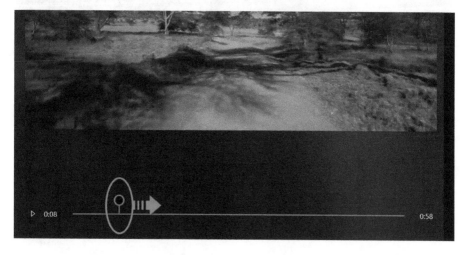

Select the 'effects' icon on the top right to reveal the effects panel, if they are not visible.

Browse through the effects listed down the right hand side of the screen.

Drag and drop the effect onto the position you want the effect to appear in the video.

In this example, I want the "impact on sand" effect to appear to the right of the dirt road.

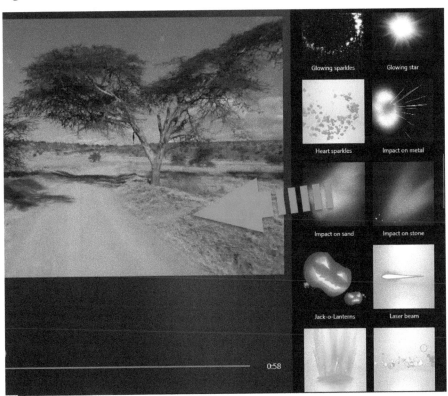

You can rotate the effect around the frame using the tree axis handles indicated with the arrows below. You can move the effect by moving the surrounding grey box and you can resize the effect using the square resize handles on the corners of the resize box.

Now to make the 3D effect more realistic, you can anchor it to a position in the video clip. Turn 'anchor to a point' to the on position.

Make sure the blue anchor on the effect is in the position you want the effect anchored to. When you play the video, the effect will stay in that position even if the camera moves.

Some of the effects have sound. You can adjust this using the volume control in the panel on the right hand side

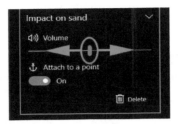

Add more effects if you want to using the drag and drop method described earlier.

You can also add effects to other parts of the clip. Scrub across your clip using the progress bar, as before. Lets add a portal.

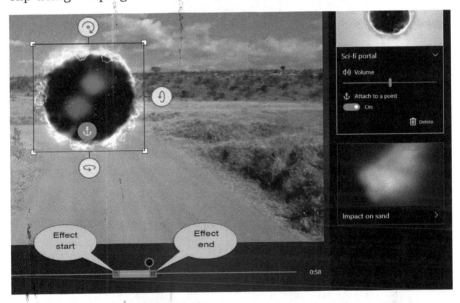

Notice below on the progress bar, you'll see a range bar appear. This will allow to adjust the duration of the effect. To adjust the range, click and drag the start and end handles, and drag them along the progress bar.

When you have added all the effects you want, click 'done' at the top right hand side of the screen.

Adding 3D Models

3D models can be added your videos. Click '3D Effects'. You can add 3D models from Microsoft's Remix library or even your own models from Paint 3D

Scrub to the part of the footage you want the effect to appear, using the progress bar underneath your video preview.

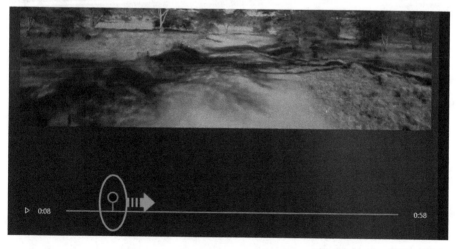

Select the '3D Models' icon on the top right to reveal the models panel, if they are not visible.

Browse through the models listed down the right hand side of the screen.

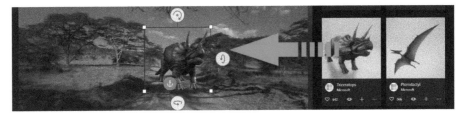

Drag and drop the model you want, onto the position you want it to appear in the video.

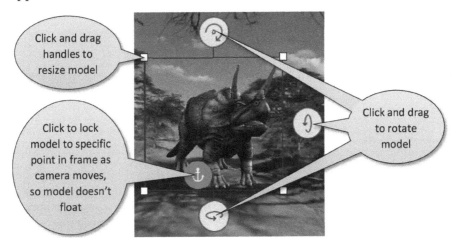

Click and drag handles to resize model

Click to lock model to specific point in frame as camera moves, so model doesn't float

Click and drag to rotate model

Use the handles to rotate, resize and position the model in the frame, as you would do for the effects we added earlier. Under the video preview window, adjust the length of time you want the model to remain on-screen. Use the beginning and end sliders as shown below. The black dot is where you are in the video, eg 58 seconds into the video clip.

Effect start

Effect end

0:58

Export & Share your Creations

You can share your creations via email or post on social media. To do this click 'export or share' on the top right of your screen.

From the popup dialog box, select the quality of your video. If you are sending the video to someone over email, select small as email doesn't support large file sizes - this is also the lowest quality.

More often than not, you'll want to share your work on social media. For this, select medium - this is better quality.

If you intend to watch on your computer click large. This is the best quality

For this example, I am going to select medium (M).

Now, to share it on social media, click 'share to social media, email or another app', on the bottom right.

From the popup menu, select a contact from the top of the list so send using 'my people' or select your favourite social media app in the section at the bottom of the popup.

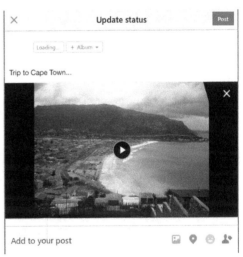

In this example, I am posting to facebook. Click 'facebook', your creation will appear in a post ready for you to add a caption.

Camera App

The camera app makes use of the on board camera on your phone or tablet to take photographs. Tap the camera app icon on your start menu to start the app.

Your tablet or phone usually has two cameras; a front facing camera, and a rear camera. The rear camera is usually higher quality and for taking photos/videos of things, while the front facing camera is usually for skype video calls and selfies.

When you start up the camera app, you'll see an image from your camera on screen.

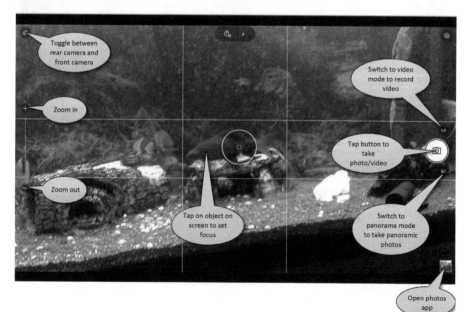

Tap on the small camera icon to take a photo.

Once you have taken your photo, you can view them by tapping/ clicking the icon on the bottom right to view in photo app.

You can also take movies by tapping on the 'switch to video' icon, on the right hand side. This works just like a video camcorder.

You can also take panoramic photos. To do this, tap the panoramic photo icon, on the right hand side. You'll see a square box appear along the centre of the screen. Point the camera at the position in the scene you want the panoramic photo to start. Tap the large white button, on the right hand side of your screen. Now, pan the camera to your right, rotating around your hips/shoulders, until you have covered the scene. You'll see the box in the centre of the screen start to build your image.

Tap the large white button again, to finish.

You can also adjust your exposure settings such as ISO, White Balance, Shutter Speed and Brightness on your camera, as well as set a timer delay. To access these settings, tap the 'pro' icon on the top of your screen.

This will reveal the exposure settings.

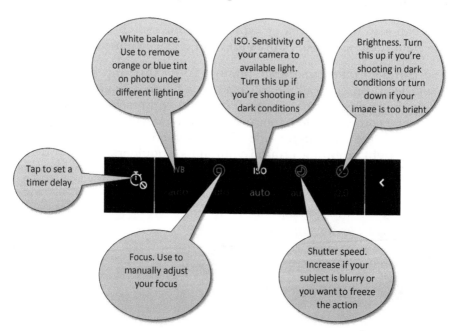

To adjust the settings, tap on one of the icons.

In this example, I am going to adjust the ISO. So tap on the ISO icon.

When you do this, you'll notice a semi-circle control appear around the 'take photo' icon, on the right hand side of your screen.

To make the adjustment, tap on 'ISO', on the right of the screen, then drag this upwards to increase the ISO, drag it downwards to decrease the ISO, as illustrated below.

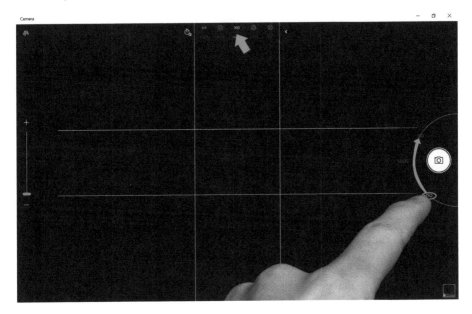

You'll see the value in the centre increase or decrease as you make your adjustment. In this example, I've set the ISO to 1600.

You can use this technique for the other settings too (white balance, focus, shutter speed and brightness).

Groove Music App

You can find the music app icon on your start menu

When you start Groove Music for the first time, it will automatically scan your computer for music and add it to your library. Click 'lets go' once the "setting things up" scan is complete.

You'll land on Groove Music's main screen. From here you can play your music, buy music from the store, or stream it to your device if you have a Music Pass. Let's take a look at the main screen.

To reveal the menu, tap the hamburger icon on the top left. ≡

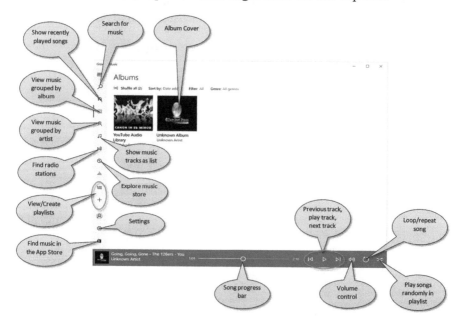

To view albums

Here you can see all the songs on this machine listed in order they were added. You can also sort them by artist and album by clicking on the links down the left hand side of the screen.

You can also buy music by clicking on the 'get music in store' link on the bottom left of the screen.

You can tap/click on a track to purchase and download it. If you are looking for a specific artist or track name, you can type it into the search field on the top right of the screen.

Groove Music Pass

A Groove Music Pass gives you access to the whole music store for a monthly subscription fee. With this pass you can stream millions of tracks directly to your device.

To apply for a pass, click the settings icon on the bottom left of the Groove Music window.

At the top of the screen tap 'get a groove music pass'

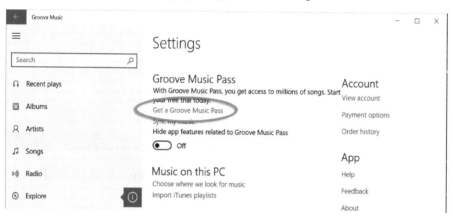

Hit subscribe on the next window, and enter your Microsoft Account username and password. You will also need some kind of payment details. Follow the instructions on the screen to enter payment details if haven't already done so.

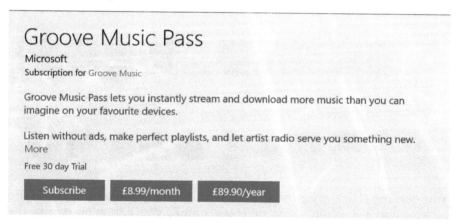

Remember you can get a 30 day trial, after that you can either pay the subscription and continue using the service, or cancel your subscription.

You can now search for any of your favourite bands, artists and albums and stream them directly to your device. Just type the names into the search field at the top of your screen.

You can add your favourites to playlists by right clicking on the track and selecting 'add to'. From the slide out menu click on a playlist, or tap 'new playlist' to create a new one.

All your playlists will appear on the left hand side of your screen.

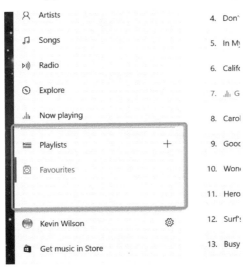

Game Mode

Game mode is designed to enhance the performance of games on Windows 10 by giving processing priority to the game. This means that more resources such as CPU and GPU processing time is given to the game, as well as more RAM and reducing the resources used by background processes and apps.

If you go to the Settings App, you'll see a new category called 'gaming'.

On the left hand side click 'game mode'. Set the slider to 'on' to enable 'Game Mode'.

Film & TV App

You can find the Film & TV app on your start menu.

With the Film & TV App you can buy/rent the latest TV shows and Films, as well as your own video content you've taken with your phone or a digital camera.

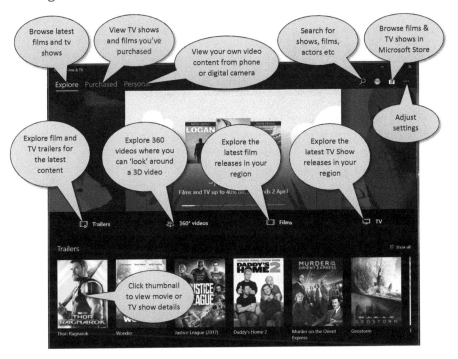

Along the top of your screen you'll see three categories: Explore, Purchased and Personal.

In the 'explore' category you'll be able to browse through the latest TV shows and Films that have been released in your region/country. You can scroll down the page and select the ones you're interested in.

In the 'purchased' category, you'll see a list of all the films and TV shows you have purchased. This is where you can select them to watch.

The 'personal' category will show you video content you have taken with your camera

Purchasing Content

Once you have found the film or TV show you want to watch, select the thumbnail cover to view the show's details

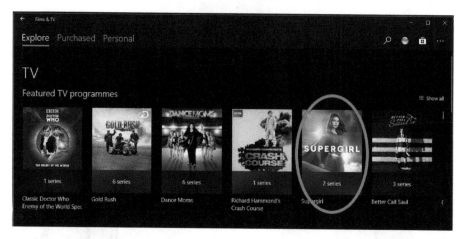

You'll be redirected to the Microsoft Store. On the store page you'll see some details about the series or film. To buy the film, or buy a whole season if it's a TV show, click the 'buy' button.

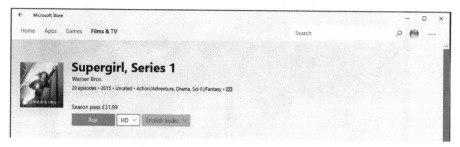

If you scroll further down the page, you'll see a description, devices you can watch the film on and in the case of TV shows different seasons.

Here you can click on the season whose episodes you want to see.

Scroll down further and you'll see a list of each episode. Here you can purchase individual episodes. To do this just click the price button next to the episode you want

Viewing Purchased Content

You'll find all the films and TV shows you have purchased in the 'purchased' section on the main screen.

Click thumbnail to play, then select an episode if you're watching a TV show.

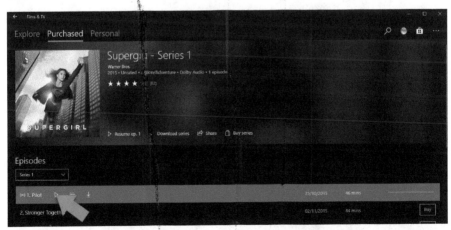

Make sure you click the little play button next to the episode title.

Search for New Content

To search for TV shows and films, click the magnifying glass icon on the top right of your screen. In the search field, type in the show's name or the film's title. Press enter.

By default, the search algorithm searches your purchased collection. To search for new content, you'll need to select 'search in microsoft store'

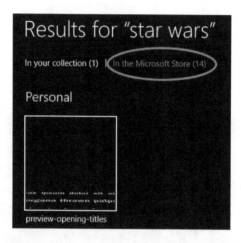

Here you'll be able to click on the thumbnails to view details and purchase the content.

Personal Content

This is where you can see the video content you have taken with your camera. Select the 'personal' category from the top of the main screen.

Along the top of the personal content window you'll see: 'video folders', 'removable storage' and 'media servers'.

Select 'video folders' to see video clips stored on your device or PC. You can also add other folders - to do this click 'add folder'.

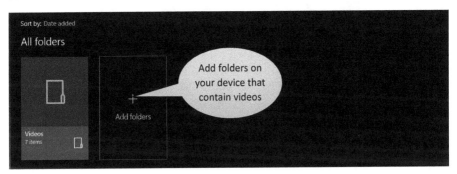

Scroll down a bit further to see all the clips in the folder.

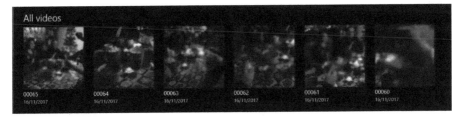

Click on one of the clips to view.

Picture-in-Picture

Also known as 'compact overlay' and allows you to watch a small video window in the corner of your screen while working in another app. In the video window, you'll see a new icon, circle below. This icon will appear in the video window on most apps as well as youtube videos in the Edge browser.

Just click this icon and the video will shrink to the top right of the screen. You can them click and drag this window to any part of your screen. I find the bottom right is a good place to put it if you're working on something else.

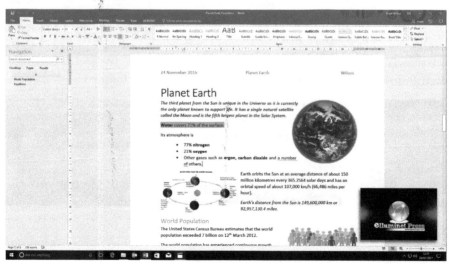

Playing DVDs

If you like watching DVDs on your PC, Windows 10 can't them out of the box, so you'll have to download a free player instead.

The best one I found is VLC media player, which can play DVDs, CDs and a range of other file types.

Just go to their website and download the software.

`www.videolan.org`

Click 'Download VLC', click 'Run' when prompted and follow the instructions on screen.

DVDs are becoming obsolete thanks to high speed internet services available to most homes and video/film streaming services that allow you to access on demand films and television programs right from the comfort of your arm chair.

Many computers, particularly laptops and mobile devices no longer include a DVD player. You can still buy external USB DVD drives if you need them.

Chapter 7

3D & Augmented Reality

Augmented Reality or sometimes called Mixed Reality, is a live view of a real world environment where computer generated sound, video and graphics are superimposed or augmented onto this real world view.

The Spring Creator's Update has a few updates to its Paint 3D app and Mixed Reality Applications.

Also some 3D capture hardware and apps for you to explore.

Paint 3D

Paint 3D is an app for creating 3D scenes and objects using a stylus pen, mouse and a keyboard and replaces the old paint app in Windows 10. You can find Paint 3D on your start menu.

Once the app has started, you'll see the welcome screen. From here you can open a blank canvas, open a saved project, or paste the contents of the clipboard into a paint canvas.

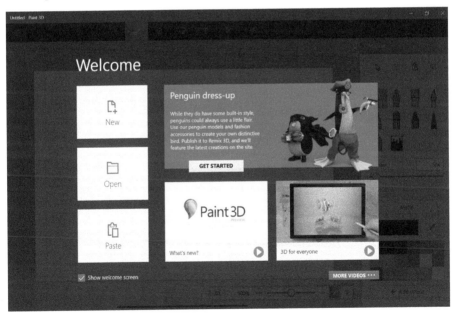

Let's create a new blank canvas. To do this click 'new'.

Chapter 7: 3D & Augmented Reality

Along the top of the window you'll find your tools. Each icon in the tool bar will open up the side panel.

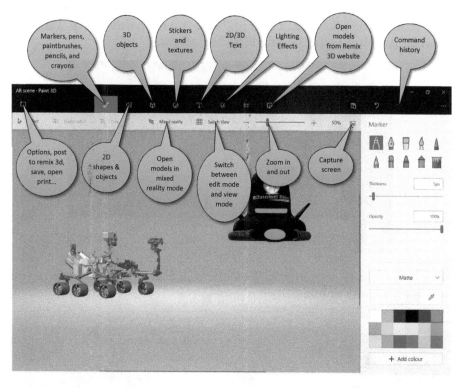

In the centre of the screen is your canvas with a control bar at the bottom that allows you to zoom in and out, edit and view your object or scene in 3D space.

Drawing

If you tap the paint brush icon, you'll see a selection of pens, pencils, crayons and markers down the right hand side of the window. Underneath you can change the thickness of the pen and select a colour.

Select a pen from the icons on the right hand side. Choose from felt marker, calligraphy writing pen, oil brush, watercolour brush, pencil, eraser, wax crayon, pixel pen, air spray and paint fill.

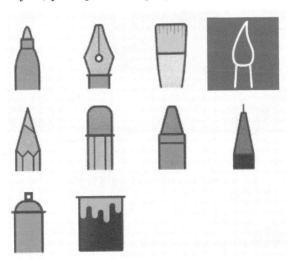

239

Adjust the thickness using the slider.

Select a finish from the drop down menu (matte, gloss, dull metal or polished metal). I'm using matte.

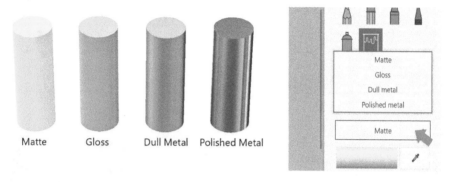

| Matte | Gloss | Dull Metal | Polished Metal |

Select a colour from the palette. If you want a colour that isn't on your palette, tap 'add colour' and select one from the colour spectrum.

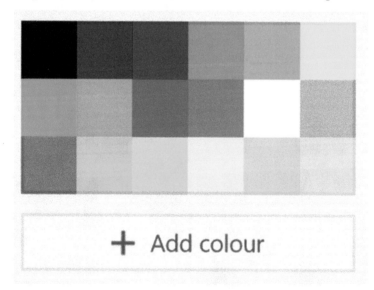

Draw directly onto the white canvas with your stylus pen or finger.

3D Objects

Tap the 3D cube logo, you'll see a selection of 3D models and objects down the right hand side of the window.

To add an object, select some from the objects section on the right hand side. In this example, I'm going to add a donut shape.

Select a finish from the drop down menu (matte, gloss, dull metal or polished metal). I'm using matte.

Select a colour from the palette.

Now, draw a diagonal line across the area on your canvas you want the object to appear.

3D Models

Tap the 3D cube logo, you'll see a selection of 3D models and objects down the right hand side of the window.

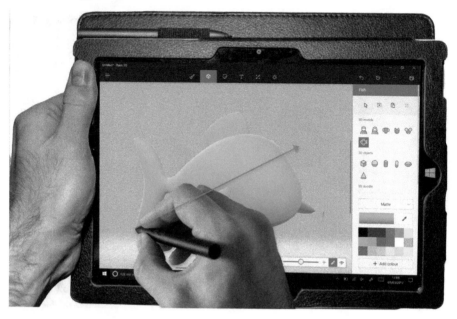

To add a model, select some from the models section on the right hand side. In this example, I'm going to add a fish model.

Select a finish from the drop down menu (matte, gloss, dull metal or polished metal). I'm using matte.

Select a colour from the palette.

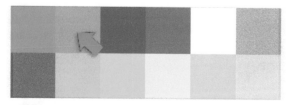

Now, draw a diagonal line across the area on your canvas you want the model to appear.

Manipulating Objects

You can rotate objects around the centre point of the object, around the vertical axis and the horizontal axis. To do this, tap on the image, you'll see a resize box appear around the object. The small white squares are the resize handles, you can tap and drag these to resize your image. Also on the edges of the resize box, you'll see four controls. These controls allow you to rotate the object. Just tap and drag these left to right or up and down.

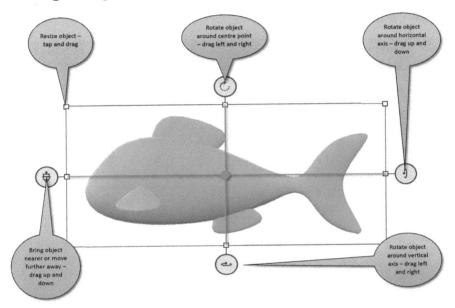

You can also move the object nearer or further away from your point of view.

2D Shapes

You can create 2D shapes such as triangles, circles, squares, stars and lines. You can create the shapes and add them to your scene, or you can stamp the 2D shape onto a 3D model.

Choose a shape from the pallet on the right hand side, tap on the canvas to create your shape. You can also add lines and curves. Tap the curve icon, then tap on the canvas to add your curve. Tap and drag the centre circle on the curve to adjust the arc. Tap the stamp icon to paste the shape in.

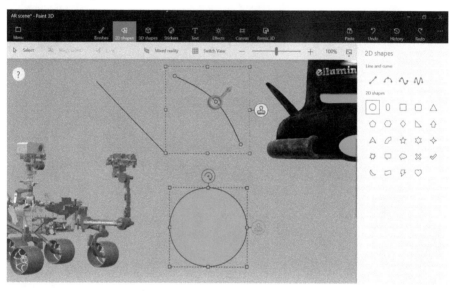

You can also pin your 2D shapes onto a 3D model. To do this, drag the shape over the 3D model, you'll notice the 2D shape will mould itself around the contours of the 3D model. Tap the stamp icon to paste the shape in position.

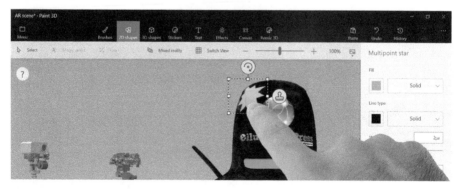

Stickers

Tap the sticker logo. Down the left hand side you'll see some sub categories.

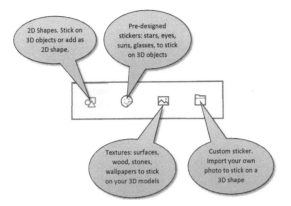

If you select pre-designed stickers from the sub category icons, underneath you'll see some stickers. For this example, I am going to add some eyes and a mouth to my fish model.

When you tap on the sticker, it will appear on your model. All you need to do is resize it using the resize handles, drag it into position, then tap the stamp icon to paste the sticker onto your model.

Custom Stickers & Textures

Tap the sticker logo. Then from the sub category icons on the right hand size, select the custom sticker icon. Tap the + to create a new sticker. From the popup window, navigate to your pictures folder and select an image.

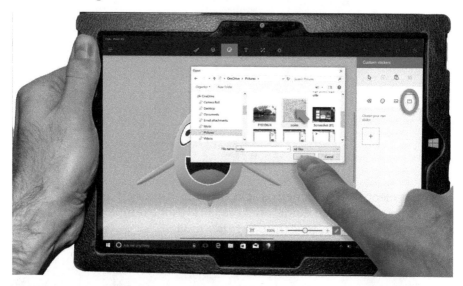

Resize your image until it covers your model using the resize handles.

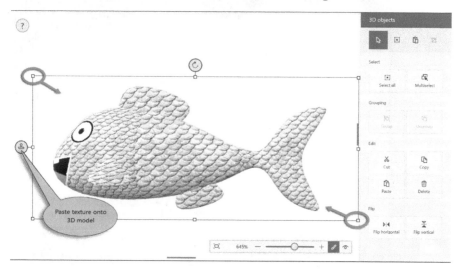

Tap the stamp icon to paste the texture to your model.

3D Doodles

Tap the 3D cube logo. You'll see, on the right hand side, a list of 3D models and objects. If you scroll down you'll see another section called 3D Doodle. The first icon converts your doodle into a 3D object with sharp edges, the second icon converts your doodle into a 3D object with soft edges.

To draw, select one of the doodle options and draw directly onto the canvas. You can only draw sections at a time, as when you start to draw on the canvas, you'll notice a light blue circle appear where you started to draw. For Paint 3D to create your 3D doodle, both your start point and end point will need to be in this light blue circle.

If you want to create a doodle with soft edges, choose the second icon from the 3D doodle section.

Again to draw your doodle, your start and end points need to be in the light blue circle.

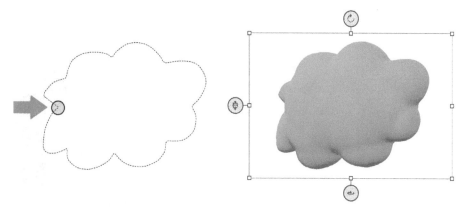

Here is an example of what you can build using simple doodles and arranging them in your 3D space.

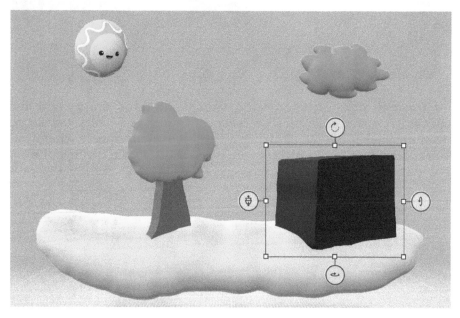

These are very simple examples to demonstrate the procedures. I can't draw and yet I can create something reasonably good, imagine what you can do!

3D Text

To insert some 3D text, select the text icon on the top of the screen. Then from the 3D text options on the right hand side, click the 3D text icon. Draw yourself a text box.

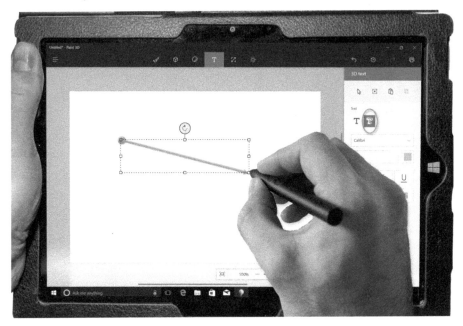

Type your text into the text box. You can change your font, size, colour and alignment, using the controls on the right hand size, as labelled below.

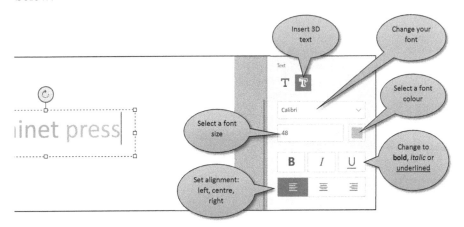

Click outside the text box to create the text.

249

You can manipulate the text as you can any other 3D object or model.

Share your Creations

You can share your creations on social media or email. To do this, click the menu icon on the far left hand side of your screen. From the drop down select 'share'. From the popup window, select where you want to share your creation.

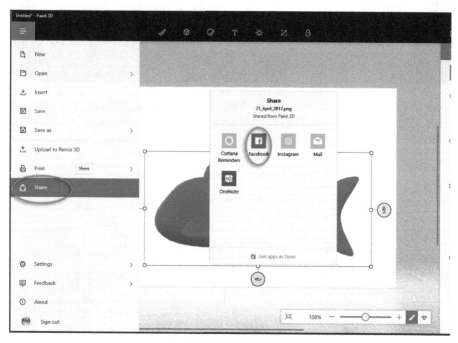

In this example, I am posting on facebook. You may need to enter your facebook login details before you can post on your timeline.

Magic Select

Magic Select is a feature that allows you to use your own photographs in a 3D scene. You can import a photograph and remove the subject from the background then paste into your scene.

For example, take our underwater scene. To insert a photo, tap the file icon on the top left of the screen, then from the backstage select 'insert'.

Browse for your file, select it, then tap 'open'.

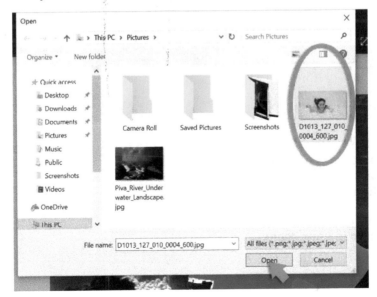

Paint 3D will paste your photograph into your scene. Now you can resize the image if you want by dragging the small white squares surrounding the image.

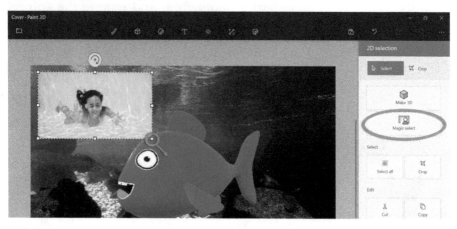

To remove the background and blend the subject in the photograph into your scene, tap 'magic select' on the right hand side of your screen.

If you look closely, you'll notice a box surrounding your photograph with 8 large white circles.

Drag these circles inwards around the subject in the photograph, as shown above. This is a mask that tells Paint 3D the part of the image you want to keep, and the part you want to discard. Tap 'next', on the right hand side. Then tap 'done'.

You can now drag the subject from the photograph you just removed anywhere in your scene.

Remix 3D site

Remix 3D is an online community where you can post your models you have created using Paint 3D.

Open your browser and navigate to the following website

`www.remix3d.com`

On the homepage, click 'sign in to remix 3D'.

Once you've signed in, you'll see two tabs at the top, 'discover' and 'my stuff'. If you click 'discover', you'll be able to browse a library of pre designed 3D models and those created by other people.

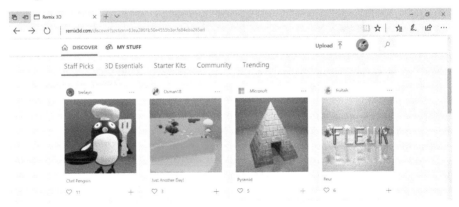

Click on the groups: 'Staff Picks', '3D Essentials', 'Starter Kits', 'Community' and 'Trending'. Have a browse through these groups to see what 3D models are available. If you see one you like, click on the thumbnail.

Then from the model information page, click 'remix in paint 3D' to open up the model.

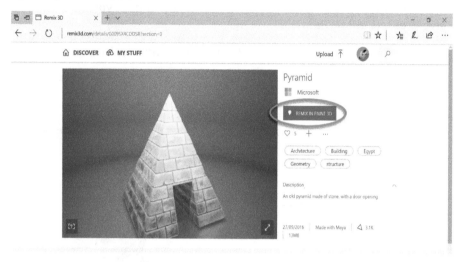

The model will open in Paint 3D, where you'll be able to edit it, resize it and add it to your scene.

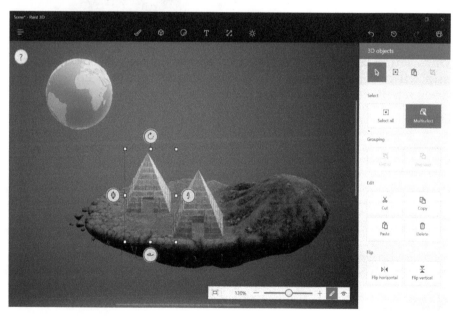

Using these objects you can build up a 3D scene.

Mixed Reality Mode

Once you have created your 3D model or built a 3D scene, you can view it in mixed reality mode, meaning you can place your work in a real world environment captured with the on-board camera on your device or headset.

To do this, tap 'mixed reality' on the top of the screen.

In the mixed reality app, you'll see your model or scene appear with a live shot from your rear camera on your device. Tap on the screen to drop the model or scene onto the live camera shot.

Tap 'Paint 3D' to go back to the Paint 3D app.

3D Builder

3D Builder is an app that allows you to build 3D models and print them out on a 3D printer. You'll find the icon on your start menu. If you can't find it, type 3D into Cortana's search field.

Along the top of the screen, you'll see some categories and some pre-designed models. Click on the models to open them.

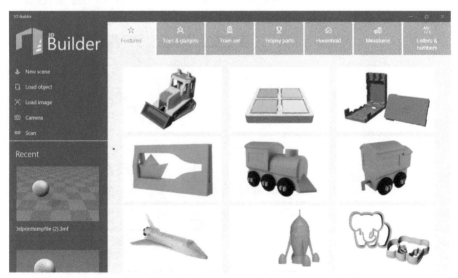

Along the left hand side, you'll see some options. Choose 'new model' to start designing an object from scratch.

Select 'load model' to open an existing model and start editing it.

Click on 'load image' to important an image and create a 3D model based on it (works best for images with high colour contrast like a black object on a white background).

Choose 'camera' to import a photo and turn it into a 3D model.

Select 'scan' to import a scan using Microsoft's Kinect device.

Scanning 3D Objects

The new 3D Scan App allows you to scan an object using the XBox Kinect sensor. If this app is not installed, you'll need to download it from the App Store. You can also use the scan option in 3D Builder.

Kinect Sensor

To start scanning objects, first, you'll need a Kinect Adapter for Xbox One S, to plug into your computer.

Plug your Kinect sensor adapter into a USB port on your computer and launch 3D Scan App or use the scan option in 3D builder.

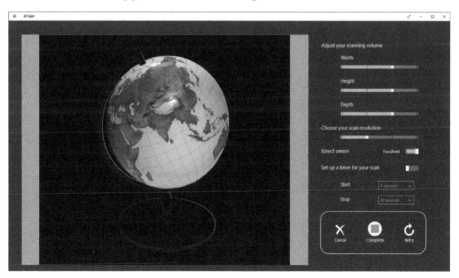

If you walk around the object you are scanning, turn the handheld mode on. If you use a turntable, put Kinect on a tripod and turn the handheld mode off.

To scan the object, it should ideally be set up on a slow turn table with a plain white or black background and the Kinect sensor mounted on a tripod or something stable, roughly 2-3 feet away.

The lighting should be diffused to minimise shadows and bright enough for the sensor to pick up clearly.

Line up the object with your Kinect sensor. Once you see the image on your screen, click 'scan', then slowly rotate the turntable 360°. You'll start to see the object build on your screen.

Click 'complete' when you're done.

You can load these scans into 3D builder for editing or 3D printing.

Mixed Reality Viewer

Mixed reality, also known as augmented reality, allows you to place any 3D model into the real world using the camera on your Windows 10 device.

With Mixed Reality Viewer, you can mix 3D models downloaded from the internet or created in Paint 3D with scenes of the real world from your on board camera. You'll find the app on your start menu

Once the app starts, you'll see the main screen with some options along the tool bar along the top.

Lets take a look...

Tap the position in the live shot where you want your model to appear.

Tap on the 'controls' icon, on the top right. Here you'll see some controls you can use to move your model, zoom in and out and so on.

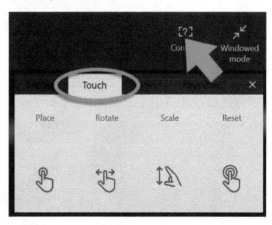

You can select different controls depending on what interface you're using. I'm using a touch screen, so I'll select the touch tab.

To scale your model, or resize it, use your forefinger and thumb - pinch the screen to make it smaller, spread your thumb and forefinger to make it bigger.

You can also rotate your model using your forefinger - just tap and drag your finger across the screen

Holographic Interface

A new component of Windows 10 is Windows Holographic, that you interact with using the HoloLens headset.

HoloLens

The HoloLens is a visor you wear over your eyes that covers your entire field of vision, and overlays digital images, 3D objects, apps and windows interface components such as your start menu, on your real world view. This is known as augmented or mixed reality.

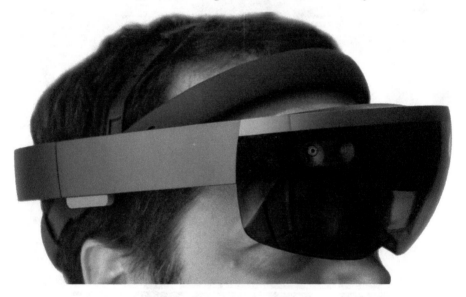

HoloLens is a completely standalone device with its own CPU and GPU.

If this is the first time turning on your HoloLens, hold the power button down for 3 seconds.

Attach the overhead strap if the headset doesn't stay secure on your head.

Put the device on your head, use the adjustment wheel on the back to tighten the headset so it fits securely around your head.

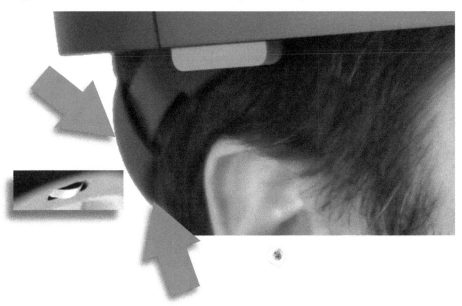

Next adjust the angle of the visor so the holographic display is centred in your view and comfortable.

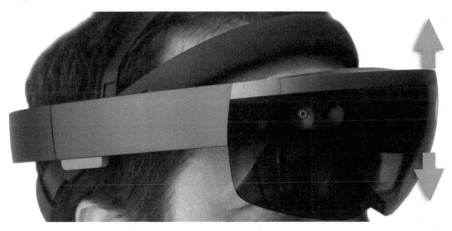

Run through the setup and calibration steps displayed on your HoloLens. Once you're happy, we can start exploring your holographic space.

Getting Around the Interface

Lets have a look at some of the basic components of the holographic interface. These are similar to Windows 10's touch-screen interface.

The Start Menu

The start menu appears when you make the bloom gesture.

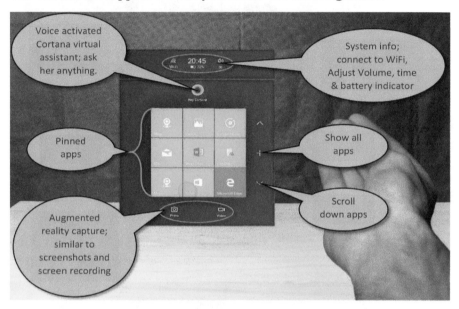

The App Bar

Also known as the 'holobar' and appears on the top of each app you launch in your holographic space.

Hololens Gestures

Much like tablets have hand gestures to manipulate objects on your screen, HoloLens has hand gestures to interact with objects in your holographic space. Lets take a look at some of the common ones.

Gesture Frame

This is the space in front of you where the sensors from the headset will detect your hand gestures in order to manipulate the holograms in your holographic space.

Gaze

The HoloLens tracks the objects you're looking at within your holographic space. This is similar to moving your mouse pointer in Windows 10. To move your cursor, you gaze or look at an object, tile or icon and 'air tap' to select it. You'll need to move your whole head rather than just your eyes.

Air Tap

This is equivalent to your left mouse button and you use it to select and manipulate objects in your holographic space. First, set your gaze on an object, then raise your forefinger and thumb and tap these two fingers together.

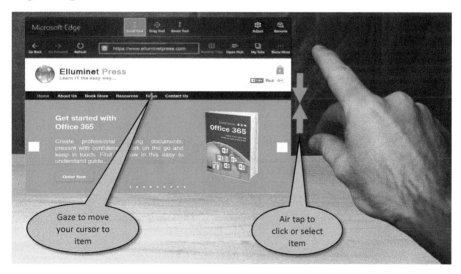

Air Tap & Hold

This is equivalent to click and drag. First, set your gaze on an object, then raise your forefinger and thumb and tap these two fingers together. While holding your thumb and forefinger together, move your hand and arm over to the position you want to drag the object.

Bloom

Returns to the start menu. It is similar to the windows key on your keyboard or clicking the start button in Windows 10. Close your hand with your finger tips together, then open your hand spreading your fingers.

 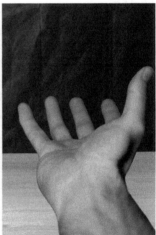

Voice Commands

The HoloLens will respond to voice commands such as

"select" instead of an air tap

"place" to place a hologram in your holographic space

"hey Cortana!" to get Cortana's attention to ask her something

"face me" to turn a hologram around so you can see it

"bigger/smaller" to change the size of holograms

So for example, gaze at an object and say "select".

Mixed Reality Headsets

There are a lot of mixed reality headsets available. Some ranging between £300-£400, such as one from Dell and Lenovo.

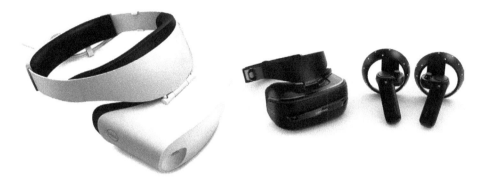

There are also other offerings from Acer which are roughly the same price.

You'll need an HDMI port on your graphics card and a USB 3 port to use most of these headsets

Windows Ink

Windows Ink will run on Windows 10 devices that are touch screen enabled. You might not find this feature on some desktop or laptop computers.

Windows Ink is integrated into apps like Maps, Microsoft Edge, Office and OneNote. As well as Windows 10's new ink work space.

These apps allow you to draw and write directly onto the screen using a pen or stylus, meaning you can annotate maps, documents, web pages, photographs, math apps and in some cases even hand writing recognition.

There are also plenty of apps appearing in the app store that support Windows Ink.

Launching Windows Ink

To launch Windows Ink, tap on the pen icon located at the bottom right of your screen.

If you don't see this icon, right click on your task bar and from the menu that appears, select 'show windows ink workspace button'.

The Windows Ink has three sections:

• Sticky Notes

• Sketch Pad

• Screen Sketch

Each of these can be found on the Ink Workspace shown below.

Sticky Notes

Sticky Notes allow you to hand write or type notes that you can pin to your desktop.

To begin writing your sticky notes, tap on the pen icon on the right hand side of your screen. From the ink space menu, tap Sticky Notes.

If this is the first time running notes, you'll be prompted to enable insights. If you enable this, Cortana will be able to interpret your notes and create reminders and read the information you write in your notes.

You can write notes, delete notes, and add new notes using the icons indicated below.

If I write 'pick up kids at 9pm', Cortana will interpret this and prompt me to add a reminder. Tap 'add reminder'.

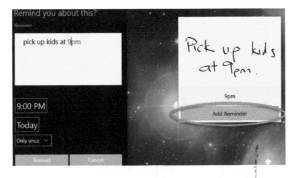

Cortana will remind you at the time you entered, and will display your reminders on your action centre in the usual way.

Sticky notes can also interpret to-do lists as well as looking up information. For example, if I am going to pick a friend up at the airport, I could write their flight number on a sticky note and use insights.

You can see below, I have written the flight number on a note and Cortana has interpreted and found a matching flight telling me the arrival time, gate and terminal number.

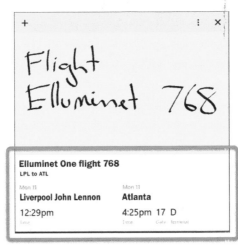

Quite a useful feature, and can also be used to look up definitions of words, stocks, exchange rates and so on. Give it a try.

Also included in Windows 10, is a sticky notes app. You can find this on your start menu. If you click on the app, your sticky notes you created in Windows Ink will appear.

Screen Sketch

With Screen Sketch, you can annotate whatever app you have open on your desktop. Just open up the app you want, then with your pen, tap the pen icon on the bottom right of your screen. Then choose Screen Sketch.

Another window will open with a screen print of your app for you to write on.

You'll see a tool bar appear on the top right of your screen. This will have all your tools such as pens and highlighters for you to use.

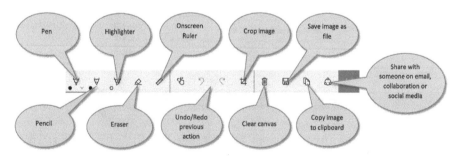

If you want to choose the pen, tap on its icon, on the tool bar. To change the colour and size, tap and hold your pen on the pen icon until a drop down menu appears. Tap on the colour and sizes you want.

Sketch Pad

Sketch Pad works like an electronic white board which could make it useful when giving presentations or teaching. You can also save and share your illustrations created while using Sketch Pad.

You'll see a tool bar appear on the top right of your screen. This will have all your tools such as pens and highlighters for you to use.

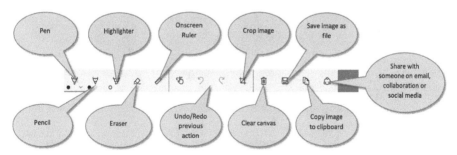

If you want to choose the pen, tap on its icon, on the tool bar. To change the colour and size, tap and hold your pen on the pen icon until a drop down menu appears. Tap on the colour and sizes you want.

Ink Apps

Right at the bottom of your ink workspace you'll see an option 'get more pen apps' or 'shop for pen apps in the store'.

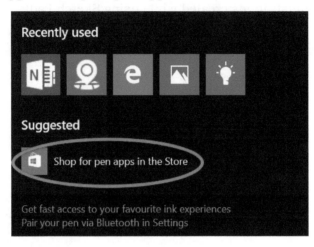

Click or tap on this option and you'll see a whole load of apps in the app store.

You'll find art apps, colouring apps, puzzles, whiteboards, notebooks, flip charts and so on. Most of these apps are free but a few of them you'll have to pay for.

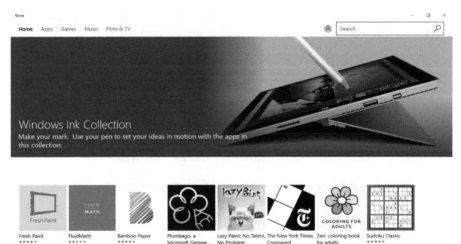

As an example, if I wanted to do some crosswords, just download and install the app in the usual way.

You can write your answers to the clues directly into the grid with your pen and the crossword puzzle will check them at the end.

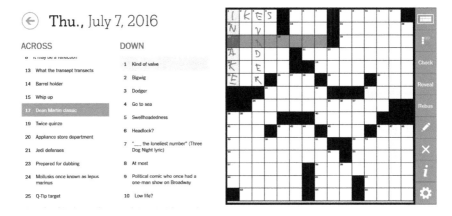

You can download art apps, that allow you to create some stunning art work and designs.

The app below is called 'freshpaint' and is a free art package that allows you to draw and paint using your pen.

OneNote & OneNote 2016 Support

Using OneNote 2016, you can use the handwriting recognition feature on the draw ribbon to convert handwritten notes into text.

Just write your notes directly onto the page using your pen.

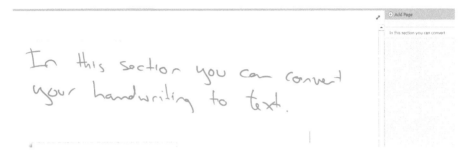

Then on the draw ribbon, tap 'ink to text'.

The conversions aren't always 100% and you'll get a few minor errors from time to time, but the software did pretty well on my handwriting.

You can always go back and edit minor errors with your keyboard.

Microsoft Word Pen Support

In Microsoft Word, you'll see an additional ribbon menu called 'draw'. This has all your drawing tools such as pens, highlighters and an eraser for you to annotate your Word documents.

Select the 'draw' ribbon and select a pen colour from the selections in the centre of the ribbon. From here you can select the colour and thickness of your pen.

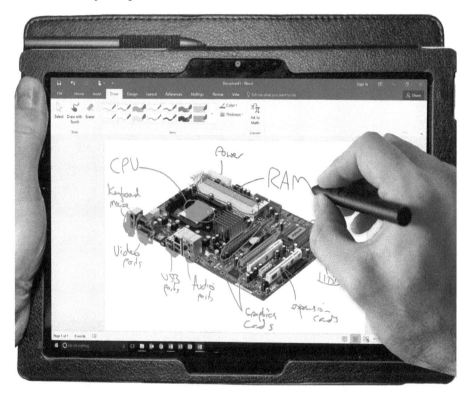

With these tools, you can draw directly onto your Word document, as shown above.

This means you can label diagrams, handwrite notes, make drawings and so on, all using your stylus or finger on your tablet.

You will then be able to save the document including all the annotations or drawings you have made.

Here you can highlight and annotate a typed Word document directly on your tablet using your stylus pen.

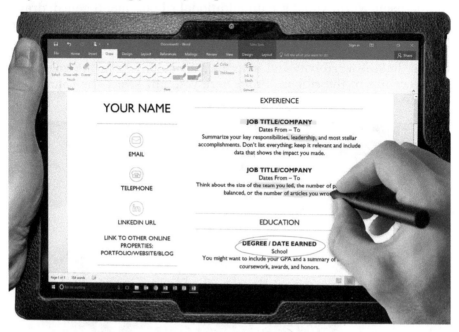

You can then save the document with all the annotations and highlights as well as share these with colleagues or friends.

Either use the share icon on the top right of your screen, or you can email the document over.

Microsoft PowerPoint Pen Support

In Microsoft PowerPoint, you'll see an additional ribbon menu called 'draw'. This has all your drawing tools such as pens, highlighters and an eraser for you to annotate your presentations.

Select the 'draw' ribbon and select a pen colour from the selections in the centre of the ribbon. From here you can select the colour and thickness of your pen.

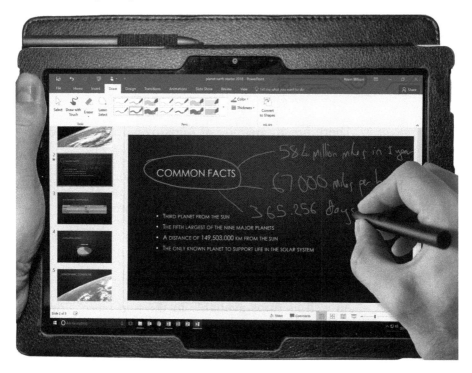

You can annotate and draw on your slides in preparation for your presentation and when you save your presentation, PowerPoint will save your drawings and annotations as well.

You can also use your pen tools while you are presenting.

All your annotations and illustrations will appear on your presentation for your audience to see.

PowerPoint will also give you an option to save your annotations added during your presentation.

Windows 10 Apps

There are thousands of Apps available for download from the App Store.

You can get an app for virtually anything, from games, entertainment to productivity apps for graphics, writing, drawing, typing and word processing.

You can download utilities such as calculators, unit converters for length, volume, currency etc.

It is definitely worth browsing through the app store.

As well as apps available in the app store, Windows comes with a few pre-installed. Such as maps, weather, news, photos, movies and music.

App Store

You can purchase and download a wide variety of Apps for productivity, games, as well as film and television programs directly from the App Store.

You can find the app store by tapping on the icon on your start menu

Once the store opens you'll come to the main screen. Here you can search for apps by typing in the name in the search field. Or you can browse through the different categories.

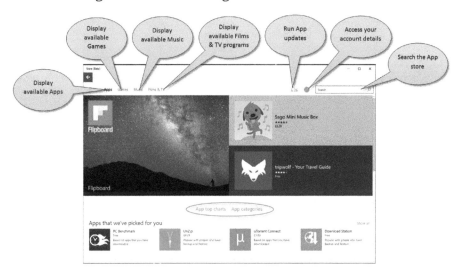

Some Apps and games you will need to pay for so you'll need to add payment details and others Apps and games are free.

If you click 'Apps' you will see a list of popular or trending apps.

Click 'App categories', circled above, and you will see a list of apps broken down in to categories such as kids and family for children's apps and things for them to do, productivity for apps such as office.

You can also search for specific types of apps by using the search field on the top right of the screen.

To buy an app, click on the App's icon to show a summary of what the app is and what it does.

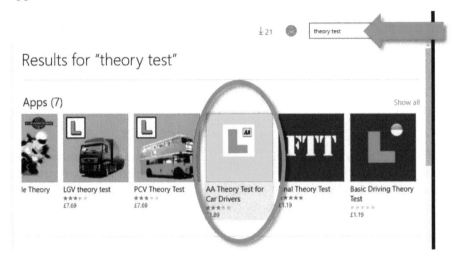

Click the price tag, circled above to purchase and download the app. You may need to enter your Microsoft Account email address and password.

Once the app has downloaded and installed, you will be able to start your app using the start menu.

Maps App

You can find the maps icon on your start menu.

The maps app is useful for exploring parts of the world, landmarks and famous places. It is also useful for finding driving directions to different locations.

You can search for pretty much any address, country, place or landmark by typing it into the search field.

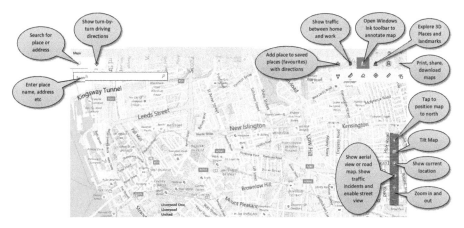

Maps App has an aerial map, and a road map. You can enable traffic flow, incident reporting, speed camera locations and street level view. To do this, select the 'map views' icon on the vertical bar on the right hand side to reveal the popup menu.

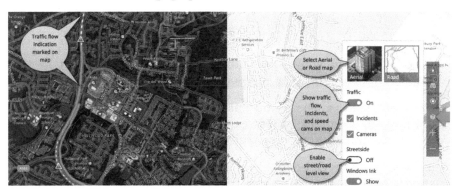

Get Directions

You can get driving directions to any location or address you can think of. You can get directions from your current location or you can enter a start location and a destination.

As well as driving directions you can get local bus routes and in some places even walking directions.

To get your driving directions, click or tap the turn-by-turn driving directions icon on the top left of your screen, labelled below.

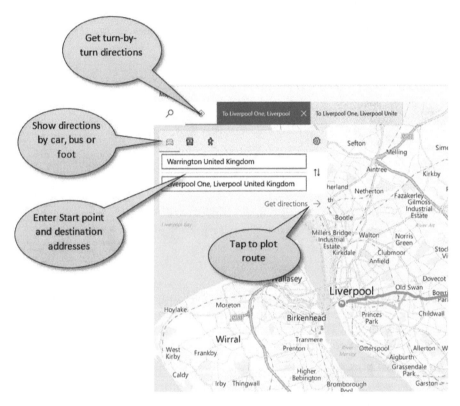

The first field will show your current location (Warrington in this example). You can also type in a location if you need to.

The second field is where you can enter your destination. Liverpool One Shopping Complex in this example. This can be a post code/zip code, residential address, town/city or place name.

Once you hit 'get directions' or tap the right arrow (next to your destination field), the maps app will calculate a route and display it on a map.

You'll see a map on the right hand side with a list of driving directions listed down the left hand side. You might see a choice of different routes, the quickest one is usually at the top.

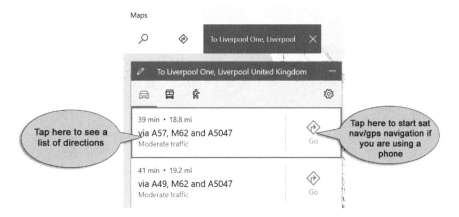

You can click on any of these directions and the map will zoom in and show you the road on the map.

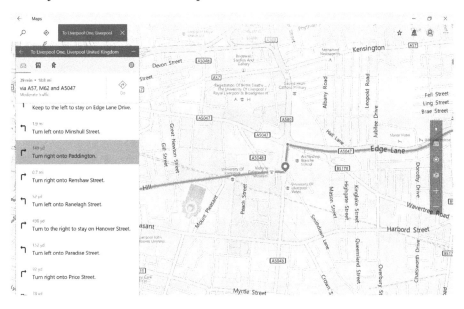

There is also an option to print the directions if needed but if you are using the maps app on your phone or tablet you can use it as a GPS or SatNav and the maps app will direct you as you drive.

Street View

Tap the maps view icon on the vertical bar on the right hand side. From the popup menu turn on 'streetside'. You'll notice some of the roads will be highlighted. Main roads and highways are in blue, minor roads are in light green. To go into street view, tap on the part of the road you want to see.

You'll see a street view of that section. To move forward, tap on a part of the road. To "look" left and right tap and drag your view to the left or right.

You can tap the part of the road you want to view on the map in the bottom pane.

Ink Directions

If I wanted to find some quick directions from my location or a specific location, to somewhere close by, I can draw directly onto the map and the Maps App will calculate a route. So in this example, I want to get from Westfield Primary School to Birch Road. Tap the Windows Ink icon, then select the directions icon from the drop down. Draw a line between your start and end points.

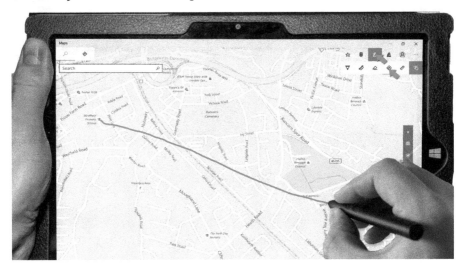

The Maps App will calculate the quickest route between your start and end points.

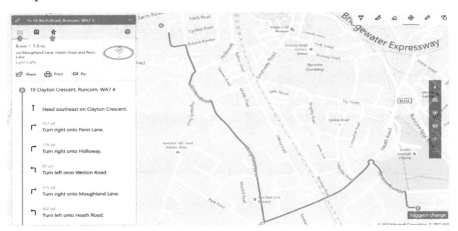

Down the left hand side, you'll see your turn-by-turn directions. Tap, the car icon for driving directions or tap, the little man icon for walking directions. Tap 'go' to start the navigation.

Measure Distances

Using the Windows Ink features, you can also measure distances between two points on the map.

Tap the Windows Ink icon, top right. Then from the drop down, select the measure tool.

Now with your pen, draw a line between the two points on the map, you want to measure.

Remember this tool doesn't take into account roads or paths on your map, just the relative length of the line you have drawn in relation to the scale of the map.

Annotations

Using the Windows Ink features, you can draw directly onto the map with your finger or pen.

Tap the Windows Ink icon, top right. Then from the drop down, select the ball-point pen tool.

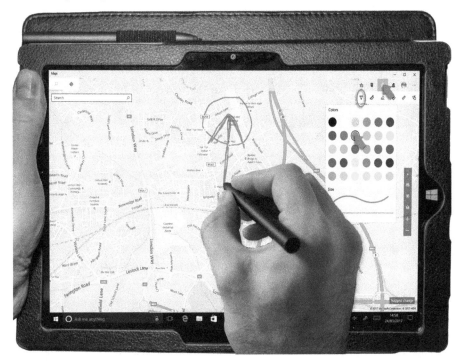

From the drop down menu, select a colour from the palette and adjust the size using the slider underneath. Drag the bar to the right to increase the thickness

Now with your pen, draw directly onto the map.

You can share these annotations with friends/colleagues or print them out.

Explore in 3D

This feature can come in hand if you want to explore landmarks or areas of interest.

You can have a look by clicking or tapping on the 'explore map in 3D' icon, circled below, and scrolling through the list down the left hand side of the screen.

Not all cities will be in 3D but the ones that are will appear in this list.

Down the left hand side you will see a number of famous landmarks and areas you can explore in 3D.

Perhaps you are going on holiday/vacation and you want to explore certain parts of the world you haven't been to - just remember the images you see aren't live and can be out of date.

Here you can see a fly-over view of a landmark. You can zoom in and out, rotate the map and move around as you explore.

Try also searching for your favourite place by typing it into the search field.

Weather App

The weather app can give you a forecast for your current location or any location you choose to view.

You can find the Weather app on your start menu. It is usually disguised as a live tile showing you weather summary for your current location.

When you first start weather app it will ask for your location, unless you have location services enabled, then it will automatically find your location.

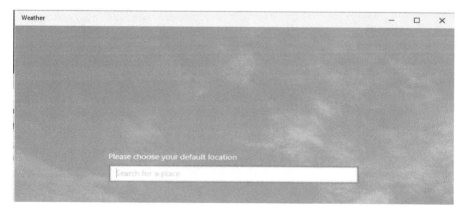

Once you have entered your location the weather app will show you a summary of the local weather conditions.

You can tap on each day to see more details, you may need to scroll down the page to see them.

Down the left hand side you have your navigation icons where you can see local weather, animated radar weather maps, historical weather and view your favourite locations list.

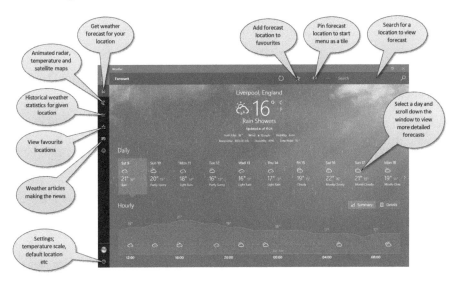

You can also find weather forecasts for other places. If for example you are going on holiday/vacation, you can enter the location's name into the search field and get a weather forecast.

You can also add forecasts for locations to your favourites list so you don't have to keep searching for them. To do this, just tap the 'add forecast location to favourites' icon along the top of your screen.

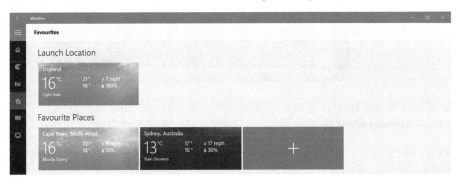

News App

You can find the news app icon on your start menu. It is usually a live tile and has up to date news headlines and images on the tile instead of an icon

The news app brings you local news headlines and stories from around the world.

Down the left hand side you have your navigation icons where you can browse different news sources such as news or sports channels.

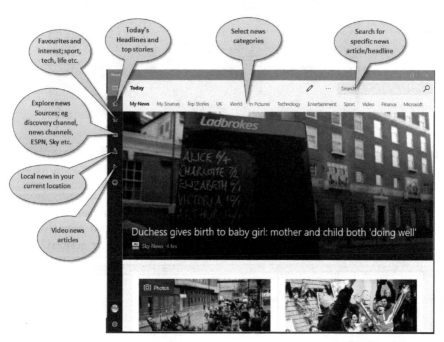

You can read the headlines, or local news, you can also watch video articles and reports.

You can find trending topics and news stories. Tap on the headlines to read the articles.

Alarms & Clock App

You can set alarms on your device, pc or phone to alert you. For example, setting a time to get up in the morning.

To do this tap the alarm tab, then tap the plus sign at the bottom of the window and enter the time.

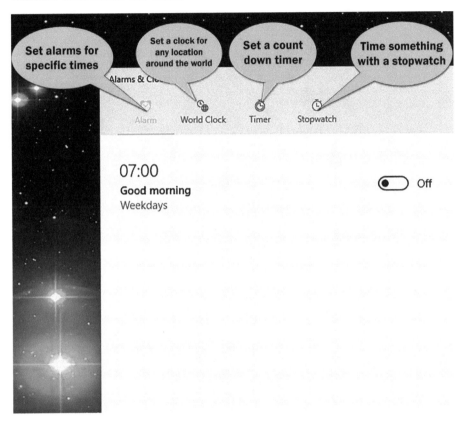

Similarly if you wanted to add a clock for another city in the world, tap 'world clock', then tap the plus sign and enter the city/country name in the search field.

This can be useful if you have colleagues or family in other countries, or just want to know what time it is there so when you skype them you aren't disturbing them in the middle of the night.

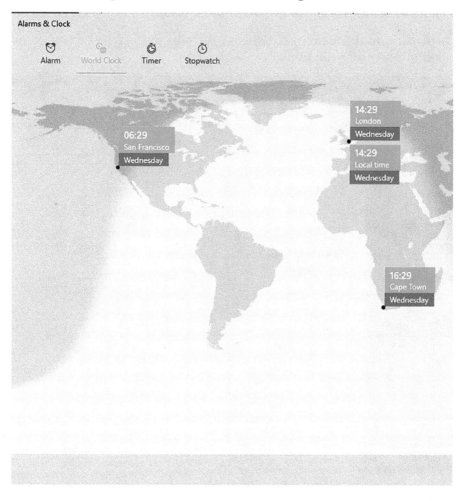

You can also create countdown timers, for example, to boil an egg for 3 minutes, time an exam for 50 minutes and so on.

Just tap timer, then tap the plus sign and enter the length of time.

Hit the play button to start the countdown.

Tap stopwatch to time something, for example, a race, lap times and so on.

Hit the play button to start the clock. Hit the flag icon to mark a lap.

Voice Recorder

Voice recorder is your on-board dictation machine. You can make voice notes, record lectures, interviews and so on. To start recording just hit the microphone icon on the screen.

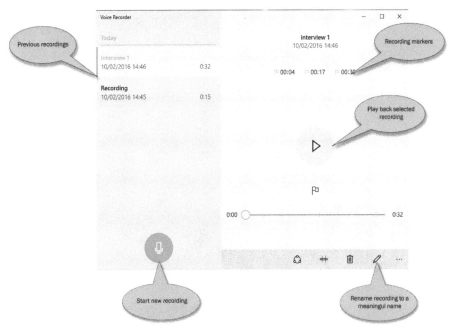

You can even add markers at important points during a recording.

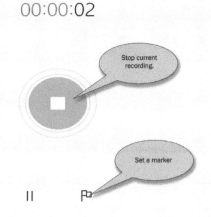

This way when you play back the recordings, you can go directly to the important points by clicking on these recording markers, illustrated in the top diagram.

297

eBooks

eBooks are now available through the App Store and can be purchased and downloaded directly to your device.

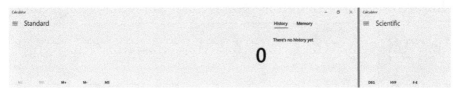

You'll see a new category called 'books', listed along the top left of the screen.

When you select the books category, you'll see a list of available books.

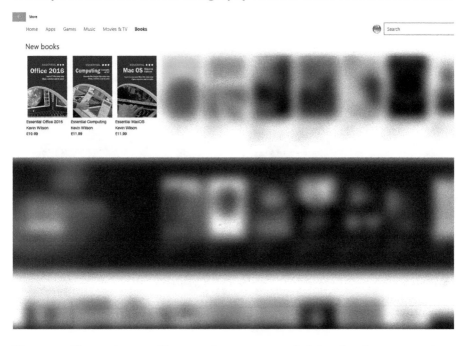

Here you'll see best sellers and recommended books from a variety of different genres. You can also browse for books in the different categories.

You can use the search field on the top right hand side of the store window, to search for a particular book title or author.

Once you have found the book you want, click the book cover.

You'll see a screen with the book's details; description, price, reviews and device compatibility.

Essential Office 2016

2016 • K. Wilson • Computers & The Internet

★★★★★ 1

£11.99

Description

Whether you're upgrading from a previous version or using it for the very first time, this book will guide you through Microsoft Office 2016 one step at a time, to help you understand the software more quickly and easily!

Techniques are illustrated systematically using photography and screen prints throughout, together with clear, concise and easy to follow text from an established expert in the field.

Whether you are new to Microsoft Office 2016, upgrading, or an experienced user needing an update, this book will provide you with a firm grasp of the underpinning foundations, and equip you with the skills needed to use Microsoft Office 2016 effectively and productively.

More

Available on

🖥️   📱
PC   Mobile

Capabilities

Text to speech
Read on up to 6 devices

Click 'buy' to purchase the book. You'll need your Microsoft Account email address and password. You may also be prompted for a payment method if you haven't added one to your Microsoft Account.

Your books will appear in Microsoft Edge Book Library.

Reading eBooks

You can now read your purchased eBooks in Microsoft Edge. To see your purchased books, click the 'hub' icon, circled below-top. Next, click the 'book shelf' icon, indicated with the red arrow below.

All the books you have purchased from the store will appear here, click on the cover to open the book.

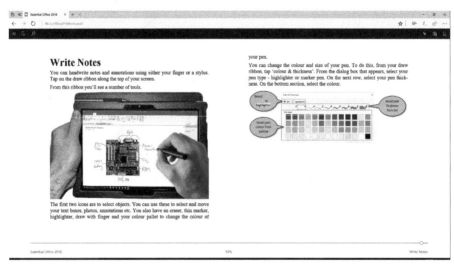

Calculator App

The calculator app works like any calculator. You'll find it on your start menu

You can choose the type of calculator you want; just a standard calculator for adding a few numbers together or a full scientific calculator for working out more complex equations.

To change the calculator click the icon on the top left of your screen, and select 'scientific'.

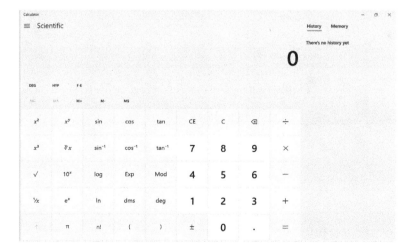

Unit Converter

You can also convert different units. You can convert between different currencies, weight, length, temperature, energy and so on. To open the converter, click the icon on the top left of your screen, shown below.

Useful if you want to convert metric measurements to ones you're familiar with. Eg: To convert from millimeters to inches, change the first one to millimeters and the second one to inches - indicated by the red arrows below.

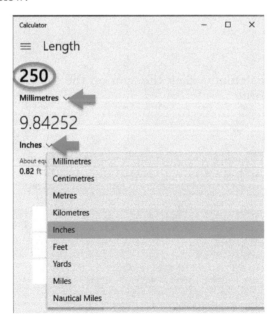

Click on the top number, circled above, usually 0 if you haven't entered anything. Now type in a value.

Currency Converter

Click the icon on the top left of your screen and select 'currency' from the drop down menu.

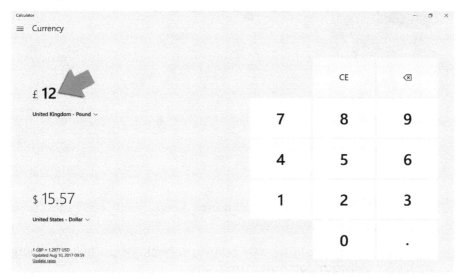

Tap on the currency numbers and enter a value using the on screen keypad, as shown above.

To change the currencies, click the currency name under the value, shown below. From the popup menu, select the currency you want.

In the example below, I'm converting from British Pounds to US Dollars.

Chapter 10

Maintaining your Computer

Computer maintenance keeps your computer in a good working order.

Using anti-virus software, backing up files, keeping your computer up to date.

Also more technical issues such as file de-fragmentation, disk clean-ups and start-up programs.

System backup and recovery procedures and advice when your PC has problems.

Here we will take a look at some common areas and procedures to keep your machine running smoothly

Anti-Virus Software

A lot of this software is sold pre-installed on the machine you buy and is offered on a subscription basis. So you have to pay to update the software. Don't buy it! There are plenty of safe free options to choose from, including Microsoft's Windows Defender Security Center.

Windows Defender

Windows 10 comes pre-installed with Windows Defender, now part of Windows Defender Security Centre, is Microsoft's free anti-virus software. It does a pretty good job at protecting your machine as is frequently updated by Microsoft.

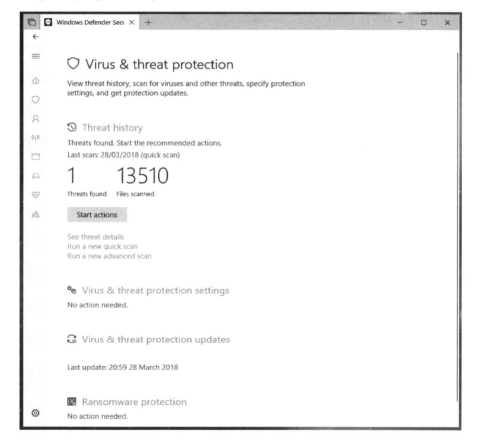

Two free ones that are a good place to start are Avast and AVG. Both of these packages are very good. The free one is basic, but you can upgrade if you need something more.

Avast

Avast scans and detects vulnerabilities in your home network, checks for program updates, scans files as you open them, emails as they come in and fixes PC performance issues.

You can download it from their website.

www.avast.com

Scroll down the page until you find 'free download'.

The other two versions here are 30 day trials and will expire after 30 days. You will need to pay a subscription to continue.

When prompted hit 'install'. If the installation doesn't run automatically, go to your downloads folder and run 'avast_free_antivirus_setup.exe', follow the on screen wizard.

AVG

AVG blocks viruses, spyware, & other malware, scans web, twitter, & facebook links and warns you of malicious attachments.

You can download it from their website.

www.avg.com

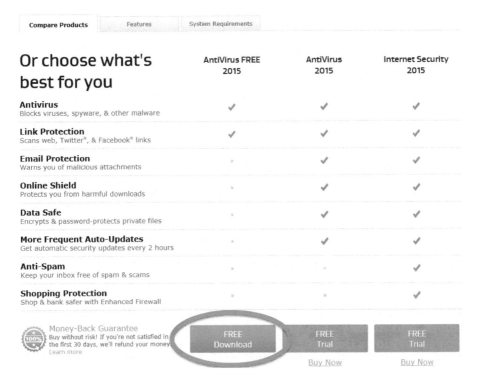

The other two versions here are 30 day trials and will expire after 30 days. You will need to pay a subscription to continue.

Security Centre

Introduced in the Creator's Update, Windows Defender Security Centre is a hub for all your Windows security features including virus protection, device health, networking, firewalls, internet security, app control and family safety options.

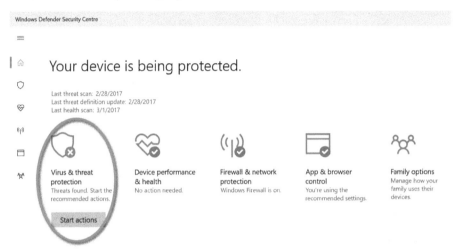

Virus & Threat Protection

From here you can launch Windows Defender or a 3rd party anti virus app. Security Centre will alert you of any potential threats, as shown above, and invite you to 'start actions' using your installed anti virus app or Windows Defender. Click 'start actions'.

From the summary page, click 'clean threats' to launch your anti virus app.

From your anti virus app, in this case Windows Defender, click 'clean pc', then from the popup, set the recommended action to 'remove' next to each detected threat, if not already done.

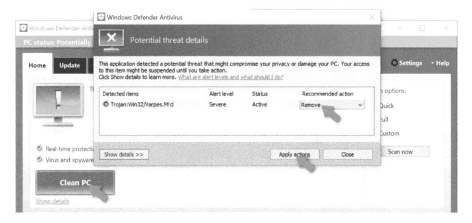

Then click 'apply actions'. This will clean your device.

Device Performance & Health

Here you can see any issues arising with drivers, updates, battery life and disk storage space. You also have the option to refresh Windows 10, meaning you can re-install Windows if it is not running smoothly while keeping your personal files safe.

Firewall & Network Protection

Here you can troubleshoot network issues with WiFi or internet connectivity and adjust your firewall settings

App & Browser Control

Here you can adjust your browser and application security settings such as SmartScreen filter that helps protect you against malicious websites, apps and downloads.

Family Options

This section links you to your family options using your web browser and allows you to monitor your kids' online activity.

Controlled Folder Access

This feature allows you to protect files & folders from modification by unapproved applications and malware. If any of these applications tries to modify files, you'll get a notification allowing you to block the action.

To enable this feature, open Windows Defender Security Center, Click 'Virus & threat protection settings', scroll down the page, then select 'Controlled folder access'.

Set the switch to 'On'.

Windows Defender will normally allow most known applications to access and change data in the folders on your machine. If Windows Defender detects an app it doesn't recognise, you'll receive a notification that it has been blocked. Some of the time this will be a legitimate application. To add other applications to the 'safe list', click 'allow an app trough controlled folder access'.

Click 'add an allowed app'.

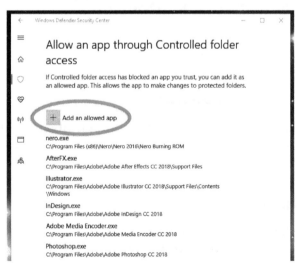

Now in the dialog box that appears, navigate to the folder where the application is installed. This will usually be "C:\Program Files". In this example, I'm going to add 'Adobe After Effects'. So navigate to the folder in 'program files'. Make sure you select the file with the EXE extension, as shown below.

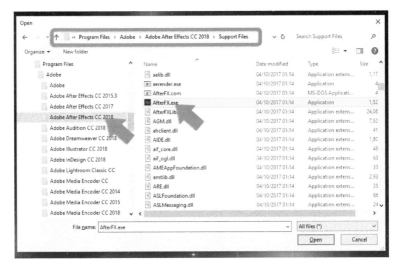

Windows Defender will automatically add your system folders and most of your personal folders. You can add any others if you need to. To do this, click 'protected folders' on the 'virus & threat protection' screen.

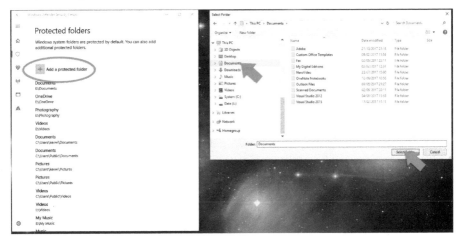

Click 'add a protected folder', then from the dialog box that appears, navigate to the folder you want to protect, click on it, then click 'select folder'.

Exploit Protection

This feature is designed to protect your PC from various types of exploits out of the box and shouldn't need any configuration.

To find this feature, open Windows Defender Security Center, click 'App & browser control' then select 'Exploit protection'.

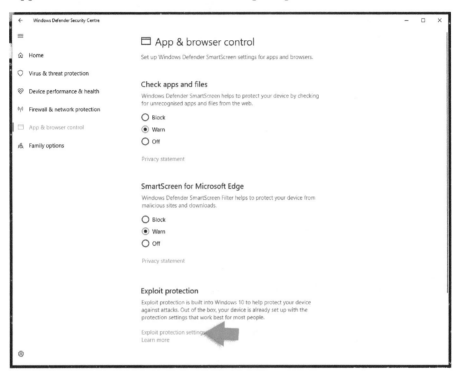

Backing Up your Files

If you have ever lost data because of a computer glitch or crash you know how frustrating it can be. So we all need a good backup strategy. I'm going to go through the strategy I have found that has worked well over the years.

Creating a Backup

First of all go buy yourself a good external hard disk. This is a small device that plugs into a USB port on your computer. Below is a typical specification for an external hard disk

Plug in your external drive into a free USB port.

In the search field on the task bar type 'file history'.

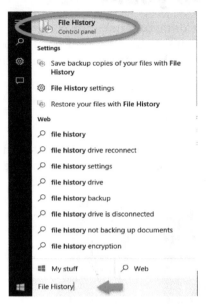

Click 'File History' in the search results, circled above.

On the screen that appears, click 'Turn On' to enable File History.

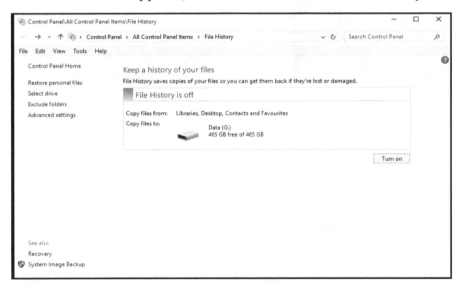

Once you have turned on File History, Windows 10 will start to copy files from your libraries (documents, pictures, music etc) onto your external hard drive.

Adding Folders

If you want to add folders to your backup, just add them to your libraries. Remember your desktop, documents, photos, music & videos folders and their contents are already included.

For example, if I wanted to include my photography folder which is on another hard drive, open file explorer, right click on the folder and go down to 'include in library'. Then from the slide-out menu, click 'create new library'.

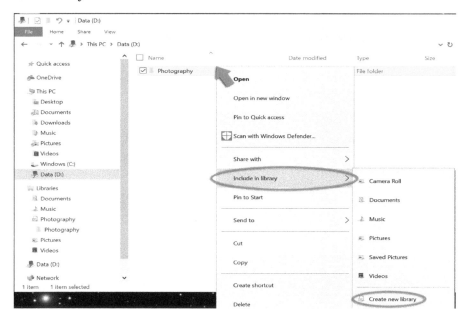

You'll see your libraries listed in the left hand pane.

This folder will now be backed up with the rest of your libraries

Setting Backup Schedules

By default, File History saves files every hour, but you can change this by clicking on "Advanced Settings" listed down the left hand side of the screen.

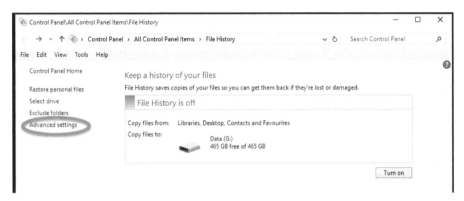

A good guide is to set how often File History saves files to "Daily". This will tell File History to save copies of your files once a day. For most users this is sufficient.

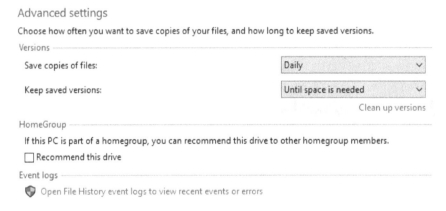

Set 'keep saved versions' to 'until space is needed'. This means that File History will keep creating backups while there is sufficient space on the hard drive, then once the drive fills up, File History will start to delete the oldest backups to make space for new backups.

Good practice would be to plug in your external drive at the end of each day to back up what you have done throughout the day.

Backups can take a while depending on how much you have done.

Restoring Files

Plug in your external Hard drive. Open up File History and click 'Restore Personal Files'

Use the left and right arrows at the bottom to navigate to the date backed up when you know your file still existed or was working.

Then in the library section double click in the folder the file was in eg pictures if you lost a photo.

Select the photo and to restore it click the green button at the bottom of the window.

317

Password Recovery

You can recover a forgotten Microsoft account password from the login screen. You'll see a "Reset password" or "I forgot my PIN" link below the password box.

Enter your Microsoft Account email address and the captcha characters, then click 'next'

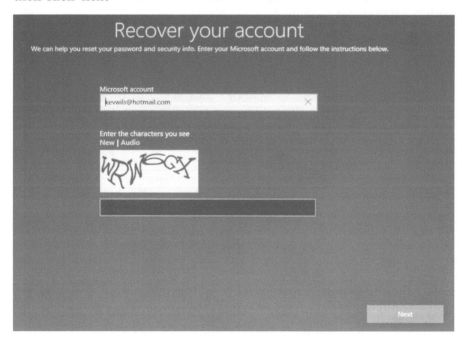

Here you'll see your recovery email address. This is the alternative email address you entered when you signed up for a Microsoft Account. Select the address reminder, indicated with red arrow below, then type the full address in the field underneath. Click 'send code'.

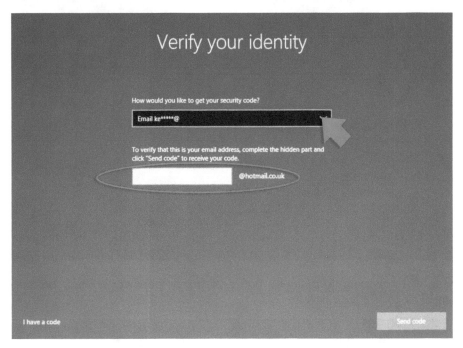

Now, log into the recovery email account and check your mail - this is the account for the email address you just entered above. You'll see an email with a code. Enter the code in the field below and click 'next'.

Enter your new password.

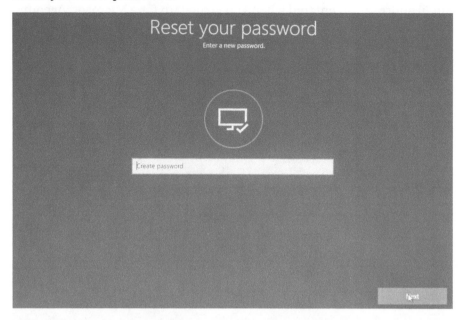

You will now be able to log on using your new password. Click 'next' to go back to the lock screen.

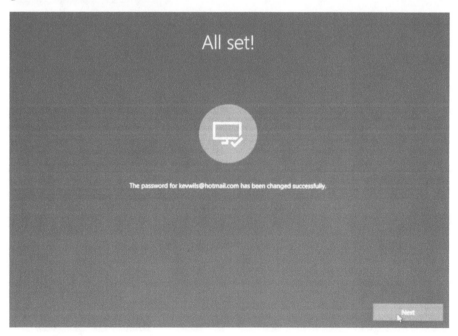

Windows Update

Windows update usually automatically downloads and installs all updates available for windows.

The Unified Update Platform or UUP allows targeted updates meaning Windows Update will only download the changes and updates included since the last update that are relevant to your version of Windows 10. This will mean smaller downloads and quicker updates.

Settings

You can find Windows Update in the Settings App on the start menu. Select 'update & recovery', then click 'windows update'.

Update & recovery
Windows Update, back-
up, recovery

Lets take a look at some of the options

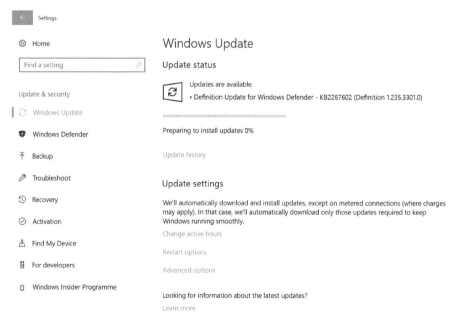

Scheduled Updates

Once Windows Update has downloaded the updates, it will schedule a system restart, if one is required to install the updates.

This is usually scheduled according to your specified 'active hours', which means Windows Update will not restart during these hours.

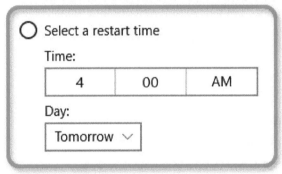

A restart has been scheduled

If you want, you can restart now. Or, you can reschedule the restart to a more convenient time. Be sure your device is plugged in at the scheduled time. The install may take 10-20 minutes.

◉ We'll schedule a restart during a time you usually don't use your device (right now 4:00 tomorrow looks good).

○ Select a restart time

Time:

| 4 | 00 | AM |

Day:

| Tomorrow ∨ |

Bandwidth Limiting

Constant updates can eat up your internet bandwidth leaving very little for you to browse the web, skype and do your work.

With this in mind, Microsoft have introduced a bandwidth limit to windows update, which means you can allocate a percentage of your bandwidth to windows update so it doesn't use your entire bandwidth to download updates

The settings for this are buried inside windows update and you can find them here..

Settings app > update & security > windows update > advanced options > delivery optimization > advanced options.

You can also find the settings using Cortana Search. Just type in...

`delivery optimization`

Click on the best match at the top of the popup box.

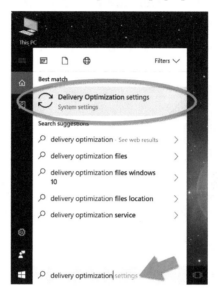

Here you can change the settings by dragging the sliders and selecting the check boxes to enable/disable limiting.

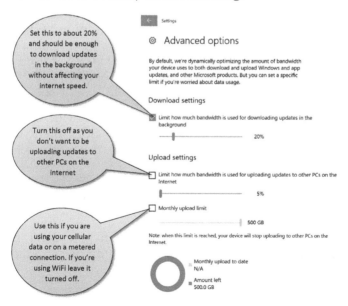

Disk De-fragmentation

Data is saved in blocks on the surface of the disk called clusters. When a computer saves your file, it writes the data to the next empty cluster on the disk, even if the clusters are not adjacent.

This allows faster performance, and usually, the disk is spinning fast enough that this has little effect on the time it takes to open the file.

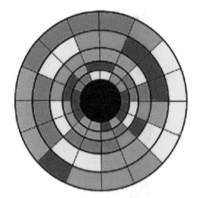

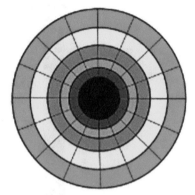

Fragmented Files   **De-Fragmented Files**

However, as more and more files are created, saved, deleted or changed, the data becomes fragmented across the surface of a disk, and it takes longer to access. This can cause problems when launching software (because it will often load many different files as it launches).

So bad fragmentation just makes every operation on the computer take longer but eventually fragmentation can cause applications to crash, hang, or even corrupt the data.

Disk defragmentation only applies to hard drives with mechanical spinning disks. If you have a solid state drive or SSD, then you don't need to worry about defragmentation and should turn off the scheduled optimisation on the drive.

It's a good rule of thumb to do this roughly once a month, to keep things running smoothly.

If you're using a solid state drive (SSD) then you don't need to defragment your drive, as it will have little effect on performance.

To de-fragment the disk in Windows 10, activate the search and type 'defragment'. Click 'Defragment and optimise your drives'.

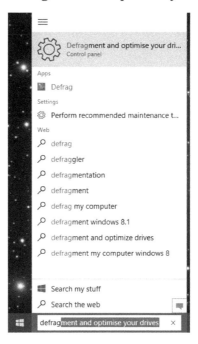

Select the drive your system is installed on, this is usually C. Click the 'optimize' button.

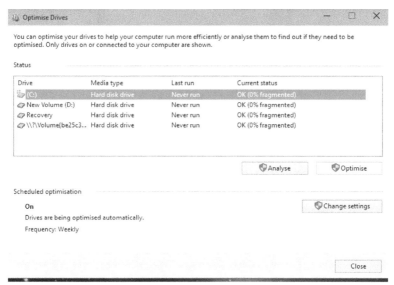

This will start de-fragmenting your disk. This process can take a while.

Disk Clean-Up

Over time, windows gets clogged up with temporary files from browsing the internet, installing and un-installing software and general every day usage. Doing this once a month will help keep things running smoothly.

Using the search on the taskbar, type 'cleanup'.

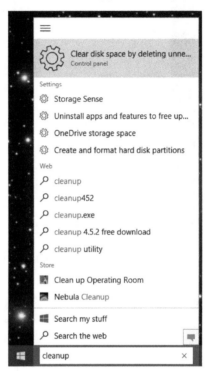

Click 'clear disk space by deleting unnecessary files'

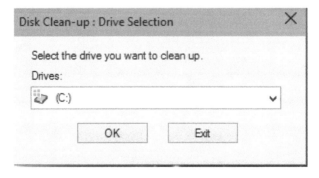

Select drive C, click ok.

In the window that appears you can see a list of all the different files and caches. It is safe to select all these for clearing.

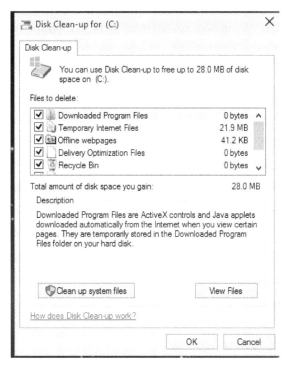

Once you are done click ok and windows will clear out all those old files.

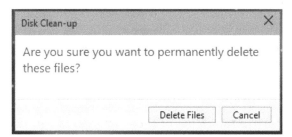

Click 'delete files' on the confirmation dialog box to clear out all the old files

Do the same with the system files. In the window above, click 'clean up system files'.

This helps to keep your system running smoothly.

A good rule of thumb is to do this about once a month.

Start-Up Programs

Start up programs automatically start when you start up Windows - this can cause Windows to become very sluggish during start up. These are usually 'helper' apps that are installed with certain pieces of software and most can be disabled without any problem.

Hit **control-alt-delete** on your keyboard and select task manager from the menu. Click more details if you don't have the screen below.

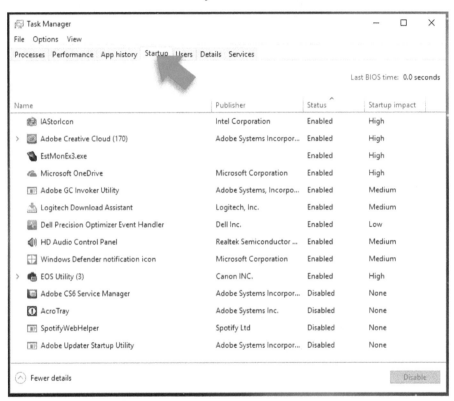

Click on the startup tab. Most of these programs can be disabled with the exception of your sound, video and network devices.

You will also see the startup impact this shows how much the program slows the machine down.

These are the programs that show up in your system tray on the bottom right hand side of your screen.

As you can see above, this system is quite clean – only essential icons appear in the tray.

Introduced in the Spring Creator's Update, you can now access start up programs from the settings app

Go to your settings app, select 'apps'. From the list on the left hand side, select 'start-up'.

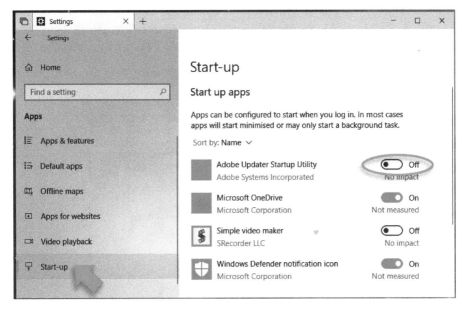

On this screen you'll see a list of apps that are configured to start when Windows starts. Click the sliders next to each app to either enable or disable them - you can turn then on or off.

Remove Programs and Apps

There are two ways you can remove programs, through the control panel or directly from the start menu.

For desktop apps such as anti-virus software, Microsoft Office, Adobe Creative Suite and similar apps, you should remove these from the 'programs and features' section of the Control Panel.

As an example, I am going to remove 'avast antivirus' from my computer.

First you need to open the 'programs and features' section of the control panel. The quickest way to do this, is to search for it using the search field on the bottom left of your task bar.

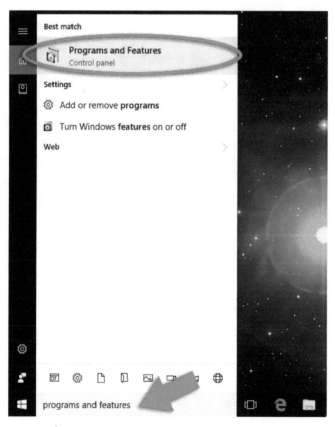

In the search field, indicated by the red arrow, type

programs and features

Click 'programs and features', circled above, from the search result.

330

Select the application you want to remove from the list, then click 'uninstall', circled below.

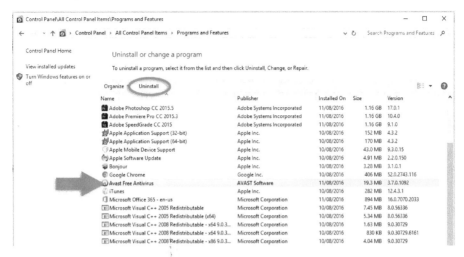

Now, depending on what program you are trying to remove, you might get a screen asking you what you want to do. In this case, avast is giving me options of what I can do.

In most cases you just have to click the 'uninstall' button, also sometimes labelled 'remove'.

Once you have done that, the install wizard will run and start to remove the software you have chosen. Depending on what you have chosen to remove, you might need to restart your PC.

Chapter 10: Maintaining your Computer

This is a similar process for removing old versions of Microsoft Office or Adobe Creative Suite and any other desktop applications.

It's good practice to go through the apps and programs installed on your device, and remove the ones you don't use anymore and any old apps. This helps to keep your device running smoothly.

For apps that you have downloaded from the App Store and ones that come with Windows 10, you can remove them directly from the start menu.

Do this by right clicking on the icon on the start menu and selecting 'uninstall'. Tap and hold your finger on the icon, if you are using a touch screen tablet.

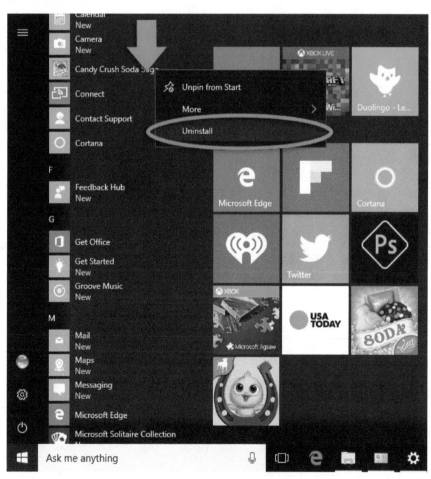

Resetting Apps

Sometimes apps can become slow and unresponsive, so in Windows 10, you have the option to reset the app. This will clear all the App's data, history lists, caches, settings and so on. This doesn't clear any of your personal files etc.

Settings App -> Apps -> Apps & Features.

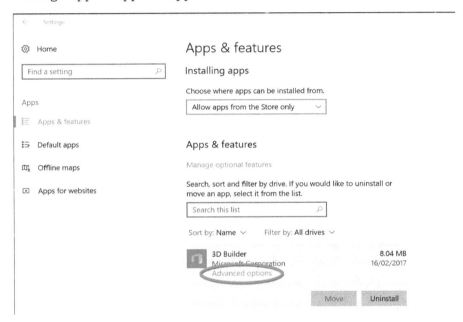

Tap on an App in the list, then tap 'advanced options'.

From the advanced options, tap 'reset'. Then tap 'reset' again to confirm.

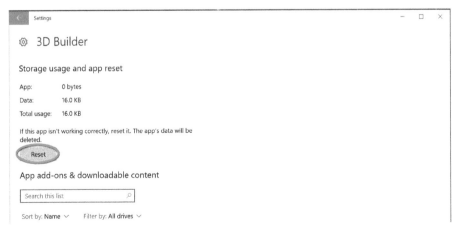

Task Manager

The task manager shows you all the processes, services and apps that are currently running on your machine, as well as some performance statistics of your processor, memory, hard drives and graphics cards. The task manager is also useful if a program stops responding and freezes up - you can terminate the program from the task manager.

To open task manager, press **control-alt-delete** on your keyboard and click 'task manager' from the options. If you see the reduced task manager as shown below, click 'more details'.

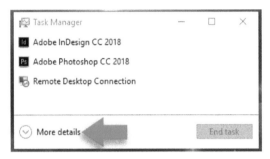

Here you will see some tabs along the top of the window. This will show you running processes, computer performance, a history of apps, apps that run at start up, apps used by a specific user, details of apps and services running.

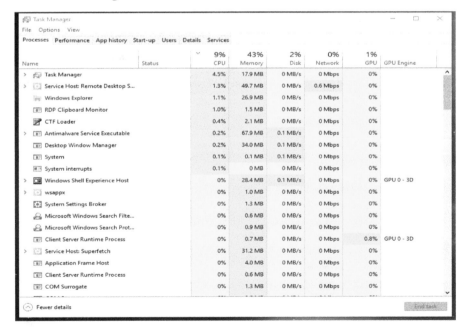

You can also terminate some of these apps - to do this click the service/app then click 'end task'. You should only do this if the particular app/service is causing a problem. Don't start terminating services as it can cause your machine to become unstable.

Task manager is useful to terminate apps that have crashed or 'not responding'.

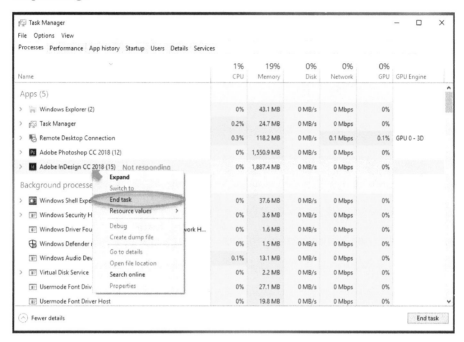

To do this, find the app in the 'processes' tab. The app that has crashed is usually marked with 'not responding'. Right click on the app and from the popup menu, select 'end task'.

You can also sort the processes according to the resources they are using. For example, if you want to see what processes are hogging all the CPU resources, click the CPU column. As you can see, the photos app is using a lot of the CPU.

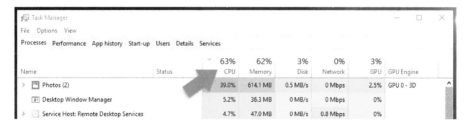

You can do the same for memory, disk, network and GPU.

Chapter 10: Maintaining your Computer

You can also check the performance of your machine. To do this select the 'performance' tab.

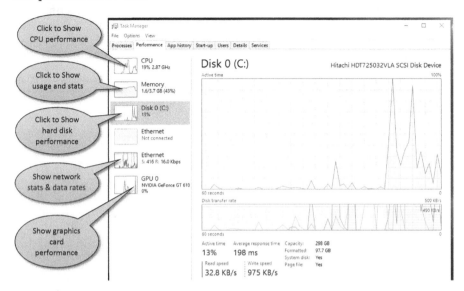

Here we can see the CPU time. On the right hand side you'll see the cores of the CPU and the graph indicates the activity - how much each core is being used to execute various tasks.

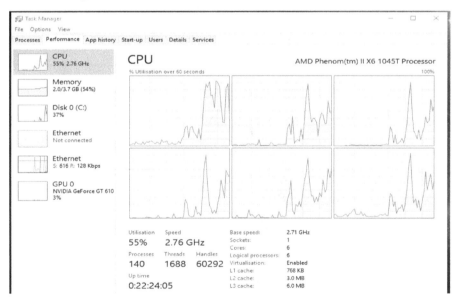

Underneath you'll see some stats for clock speed in GHz, cache sizes, cores and sockets, the up time, as well as the number of processes currently running.

System Recovery

If you are having problems then Windows 10 has a section to recover your computer.

Go to settings on your start menu.

Click update & security

Click 'restart now'

When your machine restarts, it will boot into recovery mode.

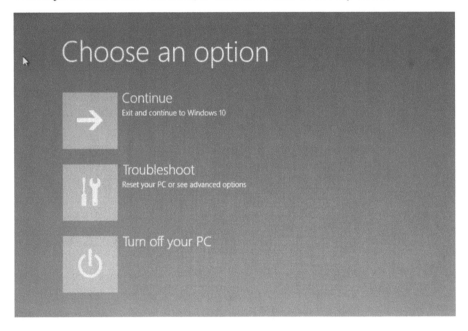

Clicking continue, will abort and return to windows 10.

Click 'troubleshoot' to enter recovery mode.

When in recovery mode you can click reset your PC.

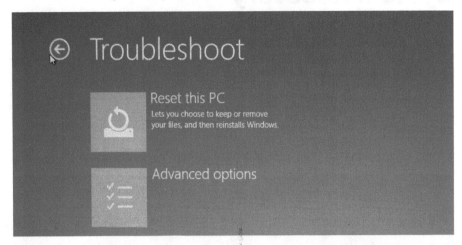

From here you can do a complete re-install by clicking on 'remove everything'. This will remove all your files and applications and reset Windows 10 back to its factory default.

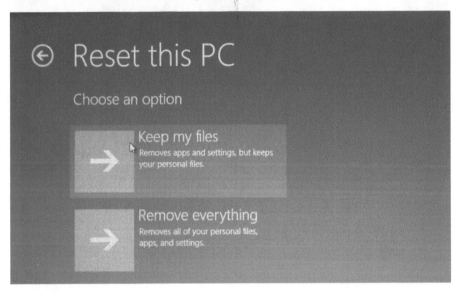

Clicking on 'keep my files', will refresh Windows 10, delete all your installed applications and settings. Your personal files and data will remain intact.

Advanced Start up

If you select 'Advanced Options' from the troubleshoot screen, there are a couple of useful features are 'system restore' which restores your PC to a previous state, for example if you installed a driver and its causing problems in windows.

Also 'System image recovery' if you created a recovery image disk. This can be used to restore windows from the image recovery disk.

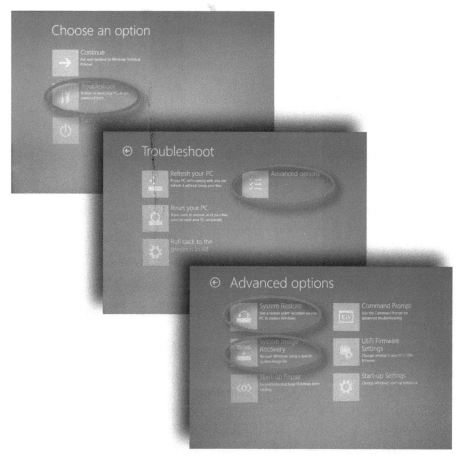

Insert your recovery disk and click 'system image recovery' to restore from a disk.

For information on creating images, see the next section.

Create a Recovery Drive

A recovery drive or recovery disk is an exact copy of your entire system often referred to as a 'system image'. This image contains your operating system (windows 10), settings/preferences as well as any applications.

This is useful if your computer crashes and you can't start it up again.

From Cortana's Search type 'backup and restore'.

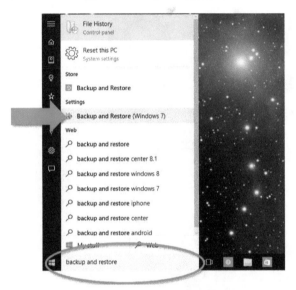

Plug in a portable hard drive (a 500GB capacity is usually more than enough).

Click 'Create a system image', then select "on a hard disk".

Click next. Make sure only 'system reserved', 'system' & 'windows recovery environment' is selected. Click next.

You will be able to start windows with this drive if your computer fails. Use the procedure outlined in 'advanced start up' in previous section.

Some Useful Utilities

Here are a couple of useful utilities I have used over the years to keep my computers running smoothly.

Piriform CCleaner

CCleaner is a utility that allows you to clear out all the rubbish such as temporary files, programs that start automatically when you log in, web caches, log files, and settings that slow your computer down.

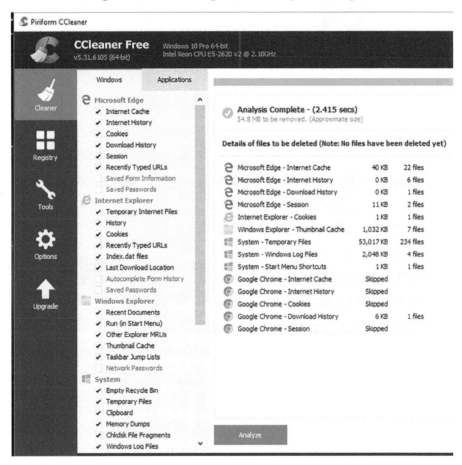

You can download the utility here...

`www.piriform.com/ccleaner/download`

Make sure you download this utility from this website ONLY and no other, as there are malware versions of this utility going around.

Malwarebytes

This utility detects and prevents contact with fake websites and malicious links. It can also detect and remove malware and is useful if your computer has become infected with some kind of adware or malware.

You can download it here...

`www.malwarebytes.com`

Click 'free download', then click 'run' when prompted by your browser.

You should NOT download this tool from any other website.

Cleaning your Computer

It's good practice to keep parts of your computer clean and in good working order.

Cleaning Keyboards

To clean your keyboard, unplug it from the computer, use a soft cloth dabbed with rubbing alcohol (or diluted washing up liquid) and run the cloth over the keys to remove all the dirt.

To clear dirt from in between the keys, a can of compressed air is a good way to do this.

Cleaning Computer Mice

First unplug your mouse from the computer.

Most mice are known as optical mice meaning they use a beam of light or a laser to track the movement. To clean these is simple.

With your paper towel use your alcohol to wipe the optical window, shown by the arrow below.

Also notice the bits of dirt circled above. Make sure you clean this with your cloth using rubbing alcohol or washing up liquid.

345

Cleaning your Monitor

Modern LCD screens can be quite fragile on the surface so take care when cleaning the screen.

First unplug your monitor from the mains power and with a soft cloth dampened with some diluted washing up liquid, start to gently wipe the surface making sure you remove dust and finger marks etc.

Dealing with Spills

If you spill liquid on a keyboard, the best thing I found to do is quickly shut down the computer, disconnect the keyboard from your computer and hold it upside down over a sink and allow the liquid to drain. If you've spilled drink on your laptop, the damage might be more serious.

If the liquid is a fizzy drink, tea or coffee, you will need to hold the keyboard on its side under warm running water to rinse off the sticky liquid - must dry thoroughly before reconnecting to your PC.

Do not do this with a laptop, notebook, tablet or advanced/wireless keyboards!!

The liquid will damage the electronics in laptops, notebooks, tablets or wireless keyboards, so these devices will need to be repaired by a professional. This can be costly.

The keyboard may not be repairable and may need to be replaced.

Fortunately keyboards are cheap now days.

The best way to avoid this situation is to keep drinks away from your laptop, computer or tablet.

Index

Index

Index

N

Near Share 86
New Message 180
News App 294
New User 52

O

OneDrive 94, 60
One Finger Slide 139
One Finger Tap 137
OneNote Support 276

P

Paint 3D 237
Pens 148
Pen Tool 155
People App 188
Photos 199
Picture-in-Picture 234
Pinch 139
Pin Contacts 190
Pin Icons to your TaskBar 81
Piriform CCleaner 342
Preview Tab 165
Print a Web Page 161
Printer Drivers 63
Printers 63
Projectors 105
Protected Folders 311
Purchasing Content 230

R

Reading Mail 179
Reading Mode 158
Recovery Drive 340
Redstone 4 16
Remix 3D 251
Remix 3D site 253
Remove Programs and Apps 330
Remove Tiles 79
Renaming Files 92
Reply to a Message 181
Resetting Apps 333

Is there no spell check ?

Index

Typed Notes 157

U

Unified Update Platform 321
Uninstall Programs and Apps 330
Unit Converter 302
Update Assistant 28
Upgrading from Windows 7 22
Upgrading from Windows 8 22
Upgrading to Windows 10 19
UUP 321

V

Verifying Accounts 45
View Ribbon 83
Virus & Threat Protection 308
Voice Commands 266
Voice Recorder 297

W

Wallet 170
Weather App 292
Web Activity 55
Web Payments 170
Whiteboard Apps 274
WiFi 49
Windows 10 Education 15
Windows 10 Enterprise 15
Windows 10 Home 15
Windows 10 Pro 15
Windows 10 Pro for Workstations 15
Windows 10 S 15
Windows Defender 305
Windows Hello 68
Windows Update 318

CPSIA information can be obtained
at www.ICGtesting.com
Printed in the USA
BVHW012230131218
535228BV00071B/630/P

9 781911 174639